JAMIE OLIVER
SIMPLY
JAMIE

Photography DAVID LOFTUS

Design JAMES VERITY

FLATIRON
BOOKS
NEW YORK

DEDICATED TO

BILL GRANGER

1969 — 2023

An effortless shining light in the culinary world, Bill's cooking epitomized charming Aussie calm, with nostalgia and a fresh lightness of touch. He was a warm, kind, wonderful man, and his influence on the food scene will be felt for years to come. Sending much love to his wife, Natalie, and his three girls. Rest in peace, dear Bill.

CONTENTS

I'M HERE TO REMIND YOU THAT YOU CAN MAKE COOKING WORK FOR YOU

By being interested in and partaking in the act of cooking, you're expressing choice and the freedom to nourish yourself and your loved ones. And it's that choice, that decision to keep cooking alive, that will forge where we go with food and farming in the next 50 years, how it evolves and develops for the future.

Whether you're a seasoned pro or just starting out in the kitchen, I want to arm you with the recipes – and the confidence – to fit more cooking into your life, with total ease.

ULTIMATELY, I WANT THIS BOOK TO INSPIRE YOU TO COOK

Right now, it seems that time is our most valuable currency. Whatever your skill level, if you're short on time, you need to be smart about how you approach mealtimes. Eating out, getting takeout or reheating something you've bought can all be convenient, but I also want to inspire you to get into the kitchen more often – and to enjoy it!

The digital revolution has turned how we access information on its head. We have instant access to numerous recipes and ideas, and endless inspiration at our fingertips, and yet we're cooking less than ever before. There's a lot of noise out there; it can be overwhelming, and volume doesn't always go hand-in-hand with trust or quality control.

That's exactly why I wrote this book – it exists to help you celebrate the simple joy of cooking. It's about reliable, achievable, fun, delicious recipes that you can work into your busy life; recipes that will give you options, and therefore control. In turn, you'll be able to thrive as a cook, and hopefully you'll be happier, healthier and save a bit of money, too.

I STILL BELIEVE THAT ANYONE CAN LEARN TO COOK

By finding recipes that are relevant to you and fit into the rhythms of your week, you'll find a way to start your food adventure or keep it going. That's why there are just five chapters here, five modern-day gears of cooking, that will work really hard for you, and ensure you're covered, seven days a week:

MIDWEEK MEALS

WEEKEND WINS

ONE-PAN DINNERS

PANTRY LOVE

DELICIOUS DESSERTS

These are recipes that can be easily adapted to suit a whole range of needs. And I've done all the hard work when it comes to ensuring that they're both nutritious and delicious, so you can feed yourself and your loved ones without worry. If you can embrace some of the principles, you'll find that these are the stepping stones to great meals and great times.

COOKING CAN REPRESENT SOME OF THE HAPPIEST MOMENTS IN YOUR LIFE

If this book inspires you to start or to keep on cooking, then I've done my job. I hope you find some ideas in here that will become a new part of your kitchen rhythms.

SIMPLY JAMIE PANTRY

As with all my recent books, I always presume you've got these five everyday staple ingredients. They pop up regularly throughout this book and aren't included in each individual ingredients list. The five heroes are olive oil for cooking; extra virgin olive oil for dressing and finishing dishes; red wine vinegar as a good all-rounder when it comes to acidity and balancing marinades, sauces and dressings; and, of course, sea salt and black pepper for seasoning to perfection.

LET'S CHAT EQUIPMENT

I tend to use a small range of equipment on repeat, so don't feel you need to spend a fortune to get kitted out in the kitchen. A set of frying pans, a couple of Dutch ovens — one shallow and one deep — and a nest of roasting pans are your key cooking vessels. Of course, a chopping board and a decent knife are a given for nearly every recipe, too. When it comes to making your life easier, a vegetable peeler, box grater and mortar and pestle are all fantastic for creating great texture and boosting flavor, and a blender and food processor will always be a bonus, especially if you're short on time.

MIDWEEK MEALS

Think easy dinners, quick fixes, shortcut ingredients, flavor bombs and working-from-home lunches. A bumper selection of recipes that will serve you well on a Tuesday night when you're tired, in a hurry, and just want something tasty to tuck into.

7 NO-COOK PASTA SAUCES

The infinite possibilities that pasta presents have always inspired me. Being able to get a delicious meal on the table in under 15 minutes when you're busy and juggling is undeniably helpful, and that's what makes these seven no-cook pasta sauce recipes so relevant. While your pasta cooks, simply zip up one of these scrumptious sauces, team them together and your mealtime is sorted. Once you embrace the no-cook sauce vibe, I'm positive it will become part of your pasta repertoire.

JARRED PEPPER PASTA

WHO KNEW SUCH BIG SUNSHINE FLAVORS COULD BE MADE SO FAST? YOU NEED THIS SUNNY ONE IN YOUR LIFE

SERVES 4

12 MINUTES

10½ oz dried penne

1 bunch of Italian
    parsley (1 oz)

1 clove of garlic

1 x 16-oz jar of roasted
    red peppers

⅔ cup blanched almonds

½–1 teaspoon dried
    red chili flakes

generous ½ cup cottage
    cheese

1 Cook the pasta according to the package instructions.

2 Blitz the parsley (stalks and all) in a blender with enough extra virgin olive oil to make a vibrant green oil, then pour into a clean glass jar.

3 Peel the garlic and place in the blender (there's no need to clean it) with the roasted red peppers (juice and all), the almonds, chili flakes, 2 tablespoons of olive oil, 1 tablespoon of red wine vinegar and half the cottage cheese. Blitz until super-smooth.

4 Drain the pasta, reserving a cupful of starchy cooking water, then return it to the saucepan. Pour over the pepper sauce and toss together over the heat, thinning with a splash of cooking water, if needed, then season to perfection with sea salt and black pepper.

5 Divide between serving plates, dot over the remaining cottage cheese, then drizzle with parsley oil to taste, keeping the rest in the fridge for up to 3 days, or freezing in an ice cube tray for future meals.

ENERGY	FAT	SAT FAT	PROTEIN	CARBS	SUGARS	SALT	FIBER
591kcal	30.6g	4.7g	18.4g	64.1g	7.2g	0.2g	1.1g

BLACK OLIVE PASTA

FOR ALL THE OLIVE LOVERS OUT THERE, THIS FAST, DELECTABLE, DELICATE PASTA IS THE ONE FOR YOU – ENJOY

SERVES 4

11 MINUTES

10½ oz dried linguine

1 clove of garlic

1¼ cups sliced black olives,
    plus extra to serve

4 sprigs of thyme, ideally lemon

2 tablespoons balsamic vinegar

1¾ oz feta cheese

1 Cook the pasta according to the package instructions.

2 Peel the garlic and place in a blender with the olives, half the thyme leaves, 1 teaspoon of black pepper, 6 tablespoons of olive oil and the balsamic. Blitz until super-smooth.

3 Drain the pasta, reserving a cupful of starchy cooking water, then return it to the saucepan. Pour over half the olive sauce (save the rest in the fridge for up to 3 days, or freeze in an ice cube tray for future meals) and toss together, thinning with a splash of cooking water, if needed.

4 Divide between serving plates, drizzle with 1 tablespoon of extra virgin olive oil, crumble over the feta and pick over the remaining thyme, then thinly slice and scatter over a few extra olives to finish.

ENERGY	FAT	SAT FAT	PROTEIN	CARBS	SUGARS	SALT	FIBER
541kcal	30.3g	5.7g	11.5g	59g	5.5g	1.7g	2.3g

BEET & RICOTTA PASTA

SHOCKINGLY VIVID, SURPRISING & FUN. MIX UP YOUR PASTA REPERTOIRE & GIVE THIS BEET NUMBER A TRY

SERVES 4

14 MINUTES

10½ oz dried farfalle

1 oz Parmesan cheese

1 lemon

½ a bunch of basil (½ oz)

9 oz cooked, vacuum-packed beets

scant ½ cup ricotta cheese

3 tablespoons walnut halves

1 Cook the pasta according to the package instructions.

2 Finely grate the Parmesan, then the lemon zest, into a blender, and squeeze in half the juice. Tear in the basil leaves, add the beets, 1 teaspoon of black pepper and 3 tablespoons of olive oil and blitz until super-smooth.

3 Drain the pasta, reserving a cupful of starchy cooking water, then return it to the saucepan. Pour over the beet sauce and toss together over the heat, thinning with a splash of cooking water, if needed, then season to perfection with sea salt and pepper.

4 Divide between serving plates, then spoon over the ricotta and crumble over the walnuts. Squeeze over the remaining lemon juice, and finish with a drizzle of extra virgin olive oil, if you like.

ENERGY	FAT	SAT FAT	PROTEIN	CARBS	SUGARS	SALT	FIBER
497kcal	21.2g	5.3g	16g	64.8g	8g	0.4g	1.4g

HERB PEA PASTA

GO BIG WITH FRESH HERBS FOR COLOR & BIG WITH LITTLE SWEET PEAS FOR FLAVOR – EMBRACE THE GREEN!

SERVES 4

11 MINUTES

10½ oz dried fusilli

2 cups frozen peas

12 green olives (with pits)

4 teaspoons capers in brine

1 big bunch of mixed soft
  herbs (2 oz), such as basil,
  chives, Italian parsley,
  mint, arugula

1½ oz Parmesan cheese,
  plus extra to serve

1 Cook the pasta according to the package instructions, adding the frozen peas for the last minute.

2 Tear the olives into a blender, discarding the pits, add the capers, tear in the herb leaves, add ¼ cup each of extra virgin olive oil and starchy pasta water, finely grate in the Parmesan, then blitz until smooth and season to perfection with sea salt and black pepper.

3 Drain the pasta and peas, reserving a cupful of starchy cooking water, then return them to the saucepan, pour over the green sauce and toss together over the heat, thinning with a splash of cooking water, if needed.

4 Serve up, finishing with a few extra scrapings of Parmesan, if you like.

ENERGY	FAT	SAT FAT	PROTEIN	CARBS	SUGARS	SALT	FIBER
502kcal	19.9g	4.6g	18.5g	66.4g	4g	1.3g	4.6g

SPEEDY SALSA SPAGHETTI

MAKING A FAST, FRESH SALSA READY TO TOSS WITH HOT PASTA IS A GAME CHANGER – IT WON'T LET YOU DOWN

SERVES 4

14 MINUTES

10½ oz dried spaghetti

1 lb ripe mixed-color tomatoes

⅓ cup mixed green & black olives (with pits)

¼ cup capers in brine

½ a clove of garlic

½ a bunch of basil (½ oz)

1½ oz Parmesan cheese, plus extra to serve

1 Cook the pasta according to the package instructions.

2 Quarter and core the tomatoes, pit the olives, then finely chop them together and place in a large bowl with the capers.

3 Peel and finely grate in the garlic, then add ¼ cup of olive oil, 1 tablespoon of red wine vinegar and a pinch of sea salt and black pepper. Tear in the basil, reserving the baby leaves, and mix well.

4 Drain the pasta, reserving a cupful of starchy cooking water, then tip it into the tomato salsa. Finely grate in the Parmesan, toss together, thinning with a splash of cooking water, if needed, then season to perfection.

5 Serve with the reserved baby basil leaves scattered over top and finish with a few good gratings of Parmesan, if you like.

ENERGY	FAT	SAT FAT	PROTEIN	CARBS	SUGARS	SALT	FIBER
573kcal	19.5g	4.3g	18g	86.6g	7.5g	1.8g	4.5g

SUN-KISSED TOMATO PASTA

ACCENTING & BLITZING A JAR OF SUN-DRIED TOMATOES IS A SUPER-QUICK, DELICIOUS HACK FOR BIG FLAVOR

SERVES 4

14 MINUTES

10½ oz dried pasta shells

1 clove of garlic

1 teaspoon dried oregano

½–1 teaspoon dried
   red chili flakes

1 x 10-oz jar of sun-dried
   tomatoes in oil

Parmesan cheese, to serve

1 Cook the pasta according to the package instructions.

2 Peel the garlic and place in a blender with the oregano, chili flakes, 1 teaspoon each of black pepper and red wine vinegar, and the sun-dried tomatoes (oil and all). Blitz until super-smooth, adding splashes of water to thin it, if needed. Tip half back into the jar and keep in the fridge for up to 3 days, or freeze in an ice cube tray for future meals.

3 Drain the pasta, reserving a cupful of starchy cooking water, then return it to the saucepan. Pour over the tomato sauce and toss together over the heat, thinning with a splash of cooking water, if needed, then season to perfection with sea salt and pepper.

4 Divide between serving plates and finish with a few gratings of Parmesan.

ENERGY	FAT	SAT FAT	PROTEIN	CARBS	SUGARS	SALT	FIBER
516kcal	28.2g	3.9g	9.6g	60.1g	3.7g	0.5g	0.7g

LEMON, ARUGULA & FAVA BEAN PASTA

SIMPLE, ELEGANT & SATISFYING, THIS IS MY KIDS' FAVORITE PASTA (MINUS THE FAVA BEANS, WHICH I LOVE!)

SERVES 4

16 MINUTES

10½ oz dried orecchiette

7 oz shelled, fresh or frozen fava beans

1 lemon

1¾ oz Parmesan cheese, plus extra to serve

3 tablespoons pine nuts

3 cups arugula

1 Cook the pasta according to the package instructions, adding the frozen or fresh fava beans for the last 4 minutes.

2 Finely grate the lemon zest into a serving bowl, then squeeze in the juice. Add 2 tablespoons of extra virgin olive oil, then finely grate in the Parmesan. Roughly crush the pine nuts in a mortar and pestle and add to the bowl.

3 Drain the pasta and beans, reserving a cupful of starchy cooking water, then add them to the bowl with the arugula, and toss together, thinning with a splash of cooking water, if needed, to create a light, creamy sauce.

4 Season to perfection with sea salt and black pepper, and finish with a few extra scrapings of Parmesan, if you like.

ENERGY	FAT	SAT FAT	PROTEIN	CARBS	SUGARS	SALT	FIBER
435kcal	15.4g	3.8g	17.1g	60.7g	2.7g	0.8g	3.5g

8 COOL WAYS WITH SALMON

EVER-POPULAR SALMON FILLETS CAN OFTEN BENEFIT FROM A MAKEOVER TO HELP KEEP THAT LOVE ALIVE

EACH COMBO SERVES 1
PREP 3 MINUTES EACH
COOK 15 MINUTES

Each combo requires **1 salmon fillet, skin on, scaled, pin-boned**. Preheat the oven to 400°F. Choose your flavor combo from the list below, rub the salmon all over with ½ a teaspoon of olive oil, prep as instructed, season with sea salt and black pepper, then place on a baking sheet lined with parchment paper. Cook for 10 minutes, or until just cooked through (or simply place in an air fryer and cook at 400°F for 7 to 10 minutes). The beauty of this is, whether you do one fillet for a solo meal or scale up to suit more people, you know that you're always going to get delicious flavor combinations. These are my family's favorites, but feel free to invent your own, too!

A Rub with a pinch of **Chinese 5-spice powder**, cover with a layer of **sesame seeds** – cook skin side down.

B Score lengthwise through the skin, stuff with **fresh soft herb leaves** – cook skin side up.

C Sprinkle with **thyme leaves**, then wrap in **prosciutto** – cook skin side down.

D Stab little holes into the salmon, poke in **rosemary leaves**, sliced **garlic** and **chili** – cook skin side down.

E Coat heavily with **Cajun seasoning**, finely smash and pat **cornflakes** all over the flesh – cook skin side up.

F Score, stuff with **mozzarella**, top with sliced **lemon**, **anchovies** and **oregano leaves** – cook skin side down.

G Top with **shaved asparagus**, **dried red chili flakes** and **sage leaves**, wrap in **pancetta** – cook skin side down.

H Score, stuff with **mozzarella**, **pesto** and **basil leaves** – cook skin side down.

ENERGY	FAT	SAT FAT	PROTEIN	CARBS	SUGARS	SALT	FIBER
306kcal	20.4g	3.4g	31.1g	0g	0g	0.7g	0.2g

THESE VALUES ARE BASED ON FLAVOR COMBO **A** ABOVE.

A

B

C

D

E

F

G

H

CRISPY NOODLE FISHCAKES

FUN, FAST & SURPRISING, TEAMING UP FISH & NOODLES CREATES THE MOST ERRATICALLY EXCITING TEXTURE

SERVES 2

18 MINUTES

1 nest of vermicelli rice
  noodles (1¾ oz)

½ a bunch of cilantro (½ oz)

2 x 5-oz white fish fillets,
  skin off, pin-boned

1 tablespoon sesame seeds

1 egg

1 lemon

2 oz soft dried apricots

2 teaspoons harissa paste

1 Scrunch and snap the noodles into a bowl, cover with boiling water and leave to rehydrate for 3 minutes, then drain, squeeze out any excess liquid, and return to the bowl.

2 Finely chop most of the cilantro on your board, saving a few leaves for garnish, then chop the fish on top into a mix of chunks and super-fine and scrape it all into the noodle bowl with the sesame seeds.

3 Crack in the egg, finely grate in half the lemon zest, add a pinch of sea salt and black pepper and scrunch together well, then divide into four and, with wet hands, shape and press into ¾-inch-thick patties.

4 Put a large non-stick frying pan on a medium-high heat and, once hot, add a thin layer of olive oil. Fry the fishcakes for 3 to 4 minutes on each side, or until beautifully golden and cooked through, then drain on paper towels.

5 In a blender, blitz the apricots and harissa with half the lemon juice and ¼ cup of boiling water until smooth, then season to perfection and spoon across two plates. Sit the crispy fishcakes on top, tear over the remaining cilantro leaves and serve with lemon wedges, for squeezing over.

ENERGY	FAT	SAT FAT	PROTEIN	CARBS	SUGARS	SALT	FIBER
416kcal	13.7g	2.3g	34g	40.1g	13.7g	1.1g	2.8g

PANTRY-RAID FISHCAKES

GRAB SOME CANS, HAVE A GOOD SCRUNCH-UP & WITHIN MINUTES YOU'LL BE READY TO FRY OFF AN EPIC BITE

SERVES 4
20 MINUTES

3½ slices of bread
(3½ oz total)

1½ x 14½-oz cans of
peeled new potatoes

1 oz Cheddar cheese

1 lemon

1 large egg

1 heaping teaspoon
English mustard

3 x 5-oz cans of tuna
in water

½ x 15½-oz can of corn

all-purpose flour, for dusting

1 Hold the bread under cold running water until completely sodden, then squeeze as hard as you can to remove excess water.

2 Tear the bread into a large bowl, drain and add the potatoes, scrunching as you go, then coarsely grate in the cheese, finely grate in the lemon zest, add the egg and mustard, season with sea salt and black pepper and mix well.

3 Drain the tuna and corn and fold through the mix, then divide into eight equal-sized balls, dust liberally with flour, and shape into patties (you can make some smaller ones for younger kids, if you like).

4 Put a large non-stick frying pan on a medium heat and, once hot, add a thin layer of olive oil. In batches, fry the fishcakes for 7 minutes, or until golden and crispy, turning halfway, then drain on paper towels.

5 Serve with a big seasonal salad and lemon wedges, for squeezing over.

AIR-FRYER IT ────────────────────

Flatten the fishcakes to ¾-inch thick, generously spritz them with oil, then cook in a single layer in an air fryer at 400°F, in batches if needed, for 12 minutes, or until golden and crispy, turning halfway.

ENERGY	FAT	SAT FAT	PROTEIN	CARBS	SUGARS	SALT	FIBER
383kcal	12.9g	3.4g	26.9g	40.1g	2.4g	1.8g	2.1g

MANGO CHUTNEY FISH BALLS

SHINY HOT BALLS ON COOL CRUNCHY CUCUMBER MAKE THE ULTIMATE IN SUPER-FUN WEEKDAY FIXES FOR THE FAM

SERVES 4 AS A STARTER
20 MINUTES

3-inch piece of ginger

9 oz white fish fillets,
    skin off, pin-boned

1 x 8½-oz package of
    cooked basmati rice

1¾ oz creamed coconut block
    or ½ cup unsweetened,
    shredded coconut

1 heaping teaspoon
    English mustard

1 egg

1 lime

1 bunch of cilantro (1 oz)

vegetable oil, for frying

2 heaping tablespoons
    mango chutney

1 English cucumber

1 Peel and roughly chop the ginger, place in a food processor with the fish, rice, creamed coconut and mustard, crack in the egg and add a pinch of sea salt and black pepper. Finely grate in the lime zest, tear in most of the cilantro (reserving a few nice leaves), then pulse until combined.

2 Now divide the mixture into 16 equal-sized pieces and, with wet hands, shape into balls. Pour ½ inch of vegetable oil into a large sturdy frying pan on a medium-high heat and, once hot, add the fish balls to cook for 8 to 10 minutes, or until golden all over and cooked through, turning regularly, and working in batches, if needed.

3 In a large bowl, thin the mango chutney with a splash of water, ready to receive the hot fish balls as they're done, carefully tossing to coat with a slotted spoon. Finely slice the cucumber, hit it up with the lime juice, and serve with the remaining cilantro leaves, for contrast.

AIR-FRYER IT

Toss the fish balls in a little oil, then cook in a single layer in an air fryer at 400°F, in batches if needed, for 12 minutes, or until golden and cooked through, shaking halfway.

ENERGY	FAT	SAT FAT	PROTEIN	CARBS	SUGARS	SALT	FIBER
279kcal	12.3g	3.5g	16.4g	26.9g	8.9g	1.1g	1.1g

SPEEDY MACKEREL SALAD

TRANSFORM EVERYDAY INGREDIENTS INTO SOMETHING ELEGANT, DECADENT & DELICIOUS IN JUST 11 MINUTES

SERVES 2

11 MINUTES

1 lemon

2 heaping tablespoons
mayonnaise

1 teaspoon English mustard

1½ x 14½-oz cans of peeled
new potatoes

2 scallions

5½ oz cooked, vacuum-packed
beets

7 oz baby spinach

2 x 3-oz smoked mackerel
fillets or smoked trout fillets

1 Quarter the lemon. Mix the mayo and mustard together to make a quick dressing, then thin with a quarter of the lemon juice and season to perfection with sea salt and black pepper.

2 Drain and roughly chop the potatoes, trim and finely slice the scallions, then, in a bowl, toss both with half the dressing to make a quick salad.

3 Slice the beets (I use a crinkle-cut knife for retro vibes) and dress with a quarter of the lemon juice, a little red wine vinegar and a drizzle of extra virgin olive oil.

4 Place a large non-stick frying pan on a medium heat with 1 tablespoon of olive oil, wilt the spinach, season to perfection and divide between plates.

5 Quickly wipe out the frying pan and return it to a low heat, cook the mackerel skin side down for 2 minutes, then flip for 1 more minute.

6 Plate up the potato salad and beets, sit the hot mackerel on the spinach, then spoon over the remaining dressing. Serve with the remaining lemon wedges, for squeezing over.

ENERGY	FAT	SAT FAT	PROTEIN	CARBS	SUGARS	SALT	FIBER
559kcal	35.7g	5.2g	22.3g	36.6g	11g	1.3g	1.4g

VIBRANT SALMON STEAMED & FLAKED

STEAMING IS FAST, HEALTHY & CREATES FRESH-TASTING FOOD READY TO RECEIVE A TASTY DYNAMIC DRESSING

SERVES 2
15 MINUTES

½ cup basmati rice

2 x 5-oz salmon fillets, skin on, scaled, pin-boned

1 baby bok choy

5½ oz broccolini

5 oz snowpeas

1 small clove of garlic

1-inch piece of ginger

1 lime

1 teaspoon sesame oil

2 tablespoons reduced-sodium soy sauce

1 tablespoon chili jam or red pepper jelly

a few sprigs of mixed soft herbs

1 Place the rice in the base of a multi-layer steamer with a pinch of sea salt, half-fill with boiling water, then bring to a boil and turn down to a medium heat. Pop the lid on for 4 minutes exactly.

2 Lay the salmon fillets in the first steamer layer, skin side down. Halve the baby bok choy and snuggle in alongside. Trim the broccolini, halving the stalks lengthwise, then place in the second steamer layer with the snowpeas.

3 Once the 4 minutes are up on the rice, stack the salmon layer on top of the base for 4 minutes with the lid on, then pop the broccolini layer on top for a final 4 minutes with the lid on. This gives the rice 12 minutes in total, and once the rice is tender the salmon and veg should also be perfectly cooked.

4 Peel the garlic and ginger, finely grate into a bowl with the lime zest, and squeeze in the juice. Add the sesame oil, soy and chili jam and mix well.

5 Drain the rice and divide between plates, arrange the greens nicely on top, then break over the salmon, discarding the skin. Drizzle over the dressing, then tear over the herb leaves, to finish.

ENERGY	FAT	SAT FAT	PROTEIN	CARBS	SUGARS	SALT	FIBER
567kcal	20.2g	3.5g	42.5g	56.6g	11.8g	1.5g	4.4g

8 DELICIOUS DRESSINGS

Mastering delicious dressings is a simple act that is absolutely key to making salads and veggies sing. And, as well as adding beautiful, often surprising flavors, olive oil-based dressings – used in moderation, of course – help you to absorb the fat-soluble vitamins that salads and veggies have to offer, so it's win-win. What follows is eight of my most-utilized dressings, and I've given you an idea for how to use each one in a fun way to get you started!

BALSAMIC DRESSING

MAKES 2/3 CUP | **2 MINUTES**

Put **1 teaspoon of Dijon mustard**, **3 tablespoons of balsamic vinegar** and 9 tablespoons of extra virgin olive oil into a glass jar. Add the leaves from **1 sprig of thyme**, then put the lid on and shake well. Season to perfection with sea salt and black pepper. Use right away, or keep in the fridge for up to 3 days, shaking well before use.

TAHINI DRESSING

MAKES 3/4 CUP | **3 MINUTES**

Squeeze the juice of **1 lemon** into a glass jar and add three times as much extra virgin olive oil. Peel and grate in **½ a clove of garlic**, add **⅓ cup of tahini**, then put the lid on and shake well. Season to perfection with sea salt and black pepper, thinning with a little water to create a drizzling consistency. Use right away, or keep in the fridge for up to 3 days, shaking well before use.

CORONATION DRESSING

MAKES 2/3 CUP | **3 MINUTES**

Squeeze the juice of **1 lime** into a blender. Seed and add **½ a green chili**, tear in the leaves from **4 sprigs of cilantro**, add **¼ cup of Greek yogurt**, **1 tablespoon of mango chutney**, **1 teaspoon each of curry powder and smoked paprika** and 2 tablespoons of olive oil, then blitz until smooth. Season to perfection with sea salt and black pepper. Use right away, or keep in the fridge for up to 3 days, shaking well before use.

GREEN GODDESS DRESSING

MAKES 1 CUP | **4 MINUTES**

Squeeze the juice of **2 limes** into a blender and add twice as much extra virgin olive oil. Halve and remove the stone from **1 ripe avocado**, then scoop in the flesh. Add **1 scallion** and **½ a green chili**, pick in the leaves from **2 sprigs of mint** and add **1 tablespoon of Greek yogurt**. Blitz until smooth. Season to perfection with sea salt and black pepper, thinning with a little water to create a drizzling consistency. Use right away, or keep in the fridge for up to 3 days, shaking well before use.

TOMATO & PEPPER DRESSING

MAKES 1¾ CUPS | 4 MINUTES

Place **1 large ripe tomato** in a blender with **2 teaspoons of jarred horseradish**, **1 large jarred roasted red pepper**, 2 tablespoons of red wine vinegar and 6 tablespoons of extra virgin olive oil, then blitz until smooth. Season to perfection with sea salt and black pepper. Use right away, or keep in the fridge for up to 3 days, shaking well before use.

CREAMY FETA DRESSING

MAKES ¾ CUP | 3 MINUTES

Squeeze the juice of **1 lemon** into a blender and add three times as much extra virgin olive oil, along with **2 tablespoons of Greek yogurt**, **1 oz of feta cheese** and **1 teaspoon of dried oregano**. Blitz until smooth and creamy. Season to perfection with sea salt and black pepper. Use right away, or keep in the fridge for up to 3 days, shaking well before use.

BEET DRESSING

MAKES ¾ CUP | 3 MINUTES

Place **3½ oz of cooked, vacuum-packed beets**, **4 sprigs of tarragon** and 2 tablespoons of red wine vinegar in a blender with 9 tablespoons of extra virgin olive oil, then blitz until smooth. Season to perfection with sea salt and black pepper, thinning with a little water to create a drizzling consistency. Use right away, or keep in the fridge for up to 3 days, shaking well before use.

FRENCH DRESSING

MAKES ¾ CUP | 2 MINUTES

Peel ½ **a clove of garlic** and finely grate into a glass jar. Add **1 tablespoon of Dijon mustard**, 3 tablespoons of red wine vinegar and 9 tablespoons of extra virgin olive oil, then put the lid on and shake well. Season to perfection with sea salt and black pepper. Use right away, or keep in the fridge for up to 3 days, shaking well before use.

LOVELY LENTIL FALAFEL

USING CANNED LENTILS & CHICKPEAS ALLOWS YOU TO QUICKLY & CONVENIENTLY MAKE THESE TASTY FRITTERS

SERVES 4

29 MINUTES

1 bunch of dill (¾ oz)

4 scallions

1 fresh red chili

2½ oz feta cheese

6½ tablespoons all-purpose flour

1 heaping teaspoon dukkah

1 x 14-oz can of brown lentils (or 1½ cups cooked lentils)

1 x 15-oz can of chickpeas

1 English cucumber

½ a small red onion

2 lemons

½ x Tahini dressing (page 42)

1 Reserving a couple of sprigs for garnish, put the dill into a food processor. Trim, roughly chop and add the scallions and chili and blitz until fine. Add the feta, flour and dukkah, drain and add the lentils and chickpeas, add a pinch of sea salt and black pepper and blitz again until combined.

2 With wet hands, divide up the mixture and roll into golfball-size rounds, flattening each slightly. Put a large non-stick frying pan on a medium heat and, once hot, add a thin layer of olive oil. Working in batches, fry the falafel for 3 minutes on each side, or until dark golden and cooked through, then drain on paper towels.

3 Peel the cucumber and finely slice into rounds, peel and finely chop the onion, then dress both with the juice of 1 lemon, a little extra virgin olive oil and seasoning, and divide between your plates.

4 Make the Tahini dressing (page 42). Divide up the falafel, drizzle over half the dressing (saving the rest in the fridge for another day), pick over the remaining dill, and serve with lemon wedges, for squeezing over.

ENERGY	FAT	SAT FAT	PROTEIN	CARBS	SUGARS	SALT	FIBER
453kcal	27g	5.8g	17g	36.7g	7.6g	1.4g	5.1g

CORONATION CHICKEN SALAD

WELCOME TO A HEARTY, FULFILLING, OPTIMISTIC SALAD FULL OF BIG, BOLD FLAVOR & INTERESTING TEXTURES

SERVES 4
23 MINUTES

2 tablespoons sliced almonds

1 x 15-oz can of pineapple
  slices in juice

1 small red onion

2 little gem lettuces

4 pappadams

1 x Coronation dressing
  (page 42)

1 lb shredded poached chicken
  (page 86)

4 sprigs of cilantro

½ a fresh green chili

optional: curry powder

1 Toast the almonds in a large frying pan on a medium heat, tossing regularly and removing once golden. Drain the pineapple, reserving the juice, then place the rings in the frying pan to get golden and caramelized on both sides.

2 Peel and very finely slice the red onion, then mix into the reserved pineapple juice with 1 tablespoon of red wine vinegar and a pinch of sea salt and set aside to quickly pickle.

3 Separate out the lettuce leaves and arrange over a large platter or plates with snapped-up pieces of pappadam.

4 Make the Coronation dressing (page 42) and add the chicken. Tear in the caramelized pineapple, mix together, and pile on top of the lettuce.

5 Drain and sprinkle over the quick-pickled onion, followed by the sliced almonds and cilantro leaves. Finely slice and scatter over the chili, add a pinch of curry powder, if you like, and serve.

ENERGY	FAT	SAT FAT	PROTEIN	CARBS	SUGARS	SALT	FIBER
399kcal	21.1g	4.8g	32.8g	19.8g	15.5g	1.3g	2.9g

GREEN GODDESS SALAD

A FEW PANTRY ITEMS & A DELICIOUS DRESSING HELP TURN A GOOD GREEN SALAD INTO A JOYFUL EXPERIENCE

SERVES 4

15 MINUTES

5 slices of bread (5 oz total)

1 clove of garlic

1½ x 6-oz jars of artichoke hearts in oil

4 eggs

2 romaine lettuces

7 oz ripe cherry tomatoes

¾ oz Parmesan cheese, plus extra to serve

2 tablespoons raw sunflower seeds

½ x Green goddess dressing (page 42)

4 sprigs of mint

1 Preheat the oven to 400°F. Cut the bread into ½-inch chunks and place in a small parchment-paper-lined roasting pan. Peel, finely chop and add the garlic, drizzle with 2 tablespoons of oil from the artichoke jar, toss well, and roast for 10 minutes, or until golden and crisp.

2 Soft-boil the eggs in a saucepan of boiling salted water for 6 minutes exactly, or cook to your liking, then drain and cool under cold running water.

3 Trim and roughly chop the lettuces and arrange over a large platter. Halve or quarter and add the tomatoes, then drain, halve and add the artichokes.

4 Finely grate the Parmesan over the croutons, scatter over the sunflower seeds, and roast for a final 3 minutes.

5 Make the Green goddess dressing (page 42), drizzle half of it over the platter (saving the rest in the fridge for another day), and gently toss to coat.

6 Peel, quarter and add the eggs, scatter over the crispy croutons and seeds, shave over extra Parmesan, if you like, and pick over the mint leaves.

ENERGY	FAT	SAT FAT	PROTEIN	CARBS	SUGARS	SALT	FIBER
392kcal	27.7g	5.8g	14.7g	21.3g	4.2g	1.2g	5.8g

QUICK GREEKISH SALAD

CRUNCHY, COLORFUL & FUN, A POP OF CRISPY CHICKPEAS ADDS AN EXTRA DIMENSION TO THIS HAPPY SALAD

**SERVES 2 AS A MAIN,
4 AS A SIDE**

17 MINUTES

1 x 15-oz can of chickpeas

1 level teaspoon
smoked paprika

1 English cucumber

11 oz ripe mixed-color
cherry tomatoes

1 red onion

12 black olives (with pits)

1 bunch of mixed mint
& Italian parsley (1 oz)

1 x Creamy feta dressing
(page 43)

1 Drain the chickpeas, put them into a non-stick frying pan on a medium-high heat with 1 tablespoon of olive oil, a pinch of sea salt and black pepper and the paprika, and cook until crispy, tossing regularly.

2 Roughly peel the cucumber, halve lengthwise and remove the seedy core. Slice ½-inch thick at an angle and put into a nice serving bowl.

3 Halve or quarter and add the tomatoes, then peel, very finely slice and add the onion. Pit and tear in the olives. Pick in the herb leaves.

4 Make the Creamy feta dressing (page 43), toss with the salad, taste, and season to perfection with sea salt and black pepper. Let the salad absorb all the lovely flavors for 5 minutes, then sprinkle over the hot crispy chickpeas and serve. Nice with flatbreads.

ENERGY	FAT	SAT FAT	PROTEIN	CARBS	SUGARS	SALT	FIBER
444kcal	28.7g	5.4g	13.8g	33.8g	14g	1.5g	10.6g

THESE VALUES ARE BASED ON SERVING 2 AS A MAIN.

DELICIOUS SEASONAL GREENS

SERVES 4 | 10 MINUTES

Toast **1 tablespoon of pine nuts** in a frying pan on a medium heat until lightly golden, tossing regularly, then remove. Trim **11 oz of seasonal green veg**, **such as broccolini or green beans**, halving any thicker broccolini stalks. Add to the frying pan and blanch in boiling salted water, giving green beans 6 minutes, and broccolini 3 minutes, or until just tender. Drain and leave to steam dry. Make the **Balsamic dressing** (page 42) and toss 3 tablespoons with the veg, saving the rest in the fridge for another day. Scatter over the toasted pine nuts. Nice hot, at room temperature, or even cold.

ENERGY	FAT	SAT FAT	PROTEIN	CARBS	SUGARS	SALT	FIBER
115kcal	9.9g	1.3g	2.8g	3.6g	2.9g	0.5g	2.8g

SIMPLE BIBB LETTUCE

SERVES 2-4 | 4 MINUTES

Remove any tatty outer leaves from **1 bibb lettuce**, then wash, gently shake or spin it dry, cut it in half and place on a nice serving plate. Finely chop and scatter over **¼ of a bunch of chives (¼ oz)**, then finely crumble over **2 tablespoons of walnut halves**. Make the **French dressing** (page 43) and drizzle ¼ cup over the lettuce, saving the rest in the fridge for another day.

ENERGY	FAT	SAT FAT	PROTEIN	CARBS	SUGARS	SALT	FIBER
240kcal	24.3g	2.9g	2.9g	2.3g	2.1g	0.5g	1.9g

EASY PASTA SALAD

SERVES 4 | 14 MINUTES

Cook **10½ oz of dried orecchiette** according to the package instructions, then drain, place under cold running water till cool, and tip into a large bowl. Meanwhile, make the **Tomato & pepper dressing** (page 43). Halve **1 English cucumber** lengthwise, use a teaspoon to remove the seedy core, then dice into ½-inch cubes. Dice **3½ oz of feta cheese** the same size. Roughly chop the leaves from **½ a bunch of Italian parsley (½ oz)**. Add it all to the pasta bowl with the dressing, toss gently to coat, then season to perfection and serve.

ENERGY	FAT	SAT FAT	PROTEIN	CARBS	SUGARS	SALT	FIBER
463kcal	19.9g	5.5g	13.8g	60.4g	5.1g	1.5g	1.4g

FUNKY POTATO SALAD

SERVES 2 | 9 MINUTES

Cook **1 lb of baby potatoes**, halving any larger ones, in a saucepan of boiling salted water for 18 minutes, or until tender, adding **2 eggs** to soft-boil for the last 6 minutes. Drain the potatoes and pop the eggs in cold water to cool while you finely slice **4 scallions** and pick the leaves from **½ a bunch of tarragon (½ oz)**. Make the **Beet dressing** (page 43) and toss with the potatoes, scallions and tarragon. Season to perfection. Peel, quarter and add the eggs. Finish with a drizzle of extra virgin olive oil and black pepper, if you like.

ENERGY	FAT	SAT FAT	PROTEIN	CARBS	SUGARS	SALT	FIBER
471kcal	29.3g	5.1g	11.6g	43.2g	5.6g	0.4g	2.8g

CRISPY BROCCOLI PANZANELLA

BORED WITH THE SAME OLD BROCCOLI? BOIL IT, SQUASH IT, COAT IT IN PARMESAN & ROAST IT UNTIL CRISPY

SERVES 2
33 MINUTES

1 head of broccoli

1½ oz Parmesan cheese

3½ oz garlic bread

½ a red onion

½ a fresh red chili

1 teaspoon capers in brine

10½ oz ripe mixed-color tomatoes

4 black olives (with pits)

½ a bunch of basil (½ oz)

1 Preheat the oven to 375°F. Peel away the tough outside of the broccoli stalk, then cut the head in half through the stalk and blanch in a large pan of boiling salted water, covered, for just 2 minutes. Drain, leave to steam dry, then use the base of a frying pan or saucepan to gently squash each half to about ¾-inch thick.

2 Line a roasting pan with parchment paper, rub with a little olive oil and finely grate over half the Parmesan in an even layer, covering enough space to sit the broccoli halves on top, cut side down. Finely grate over the remaining Parmesan to generously cover the broccoli and roast for 20 minutes, or until golden and crispy, cooking the garlic bread alongside.

3 Peel the onion and finely chop with the chili, then place in a bowl with the capers. Halve or quarter and add the tomatoes, then pit and tear in the olives. Tear in most of the basil leaves, reserving a few for garnish, then dress with 1 tablespoon of red wine vinegar and 2 tablespoons of extra virgin olive oil. Leave to marinate.

4 Once done, tear or cut the garlic bread into little chunks, scrunch into the salad, season to perfection and divide between plates. Flip the broccoli, revealing its crispy bottom, and sit it on top. Sprinkle with the reserved basil leaves and any leftover crispy Parmesan bits.

ENERGY	FAT	SAT FAT	PROTEIN	CARBS	SUGARS	SALT	FIBER
326kcal	33.3g	11g	21.8g	37.4g	12.9g	1.5g	11.5g

UPSIDE-DOWN NOODLE RICE BOWL

CONTRASTING SIMPLE NOODLES, RICE & VEG WITH OOZY SPICED EGGS & TANGY SICHUAN CHILI OIL IS A REAL JOY

SERVES 2

18 MINUTES

1 nest of vermicelli
    rice noodles (1¾ oz)

sesame oil

1 package (10–12 oz) of
    mixed fresh stir-fry veg

3 tablespoons unsalted
    cashews

2 tablespoons reduced-sodium
    soy sauce

1 x 8½-oz package of cooked
    brown rice

2 limes

2 eggs

curry powder

Sichuan or chili crisp oil

½ a bunch of cilantro (½ oz)

1 Rehydrate the noodles in a deep 7-inch serving bowl according to the package instructions, then drain, return to the bowl and toss in a little sesame oil.

2 Tip the stir-fry veg into a very hot large non-stick frying pan with a little olive oil and the cashews and fry for 4 minutes, or until just tender, tossing regularly. Season to perfection with the soy, then pile the veg into the bowl on top of the noodles.

3 Crumble the rice into the same frying pan, squeezing over the juice of 1 lime. Once hot, layer on top of the veg and press down with a slotted spatula to compact.

4 Quickly wipe out the frying pan and place back on a medium heat. Drizzle in 2 tablespoons of olive oil, crack in the eggs and season with a pinch of sea salt and black pepper, then dust with curry powder. Cook to your liking, spooning over the hot oil as they cook.

5 Turn out the bowl (like a sandcastle!), top with the spiced fried eggs, spoon over Sichuan chili oil to taste, and pick over the cilantro leaves. Squeeze over the remaining lime juice and serve.

ENERGY	FAT	SAT FAT	PROTEIN	CARBS	SUGARS	SALT	FIBER
593kcal	32.7g	5.8g	15.8g	48.2g	8.6g	1.8g	8.6g

STICKY MISO EGGPLANT

BOILING, STEAMING & FRYING THE EGGPLANT CREATES THE MOST AMAZING TEXTURE – THIS ONE IS A DELIGHT

SERVES 2
20 MINUTES

1 large eggplant

¾ cup basmati rice

2 tablespoons unsweetened
    shredded coconut

1 lime

1 heaping tablespoon miso

1 tablespoon reduced-sodium
    soy sauce

1 tablespoon liquid honey

1 tablespoon rice wine vinegar

1 tablespoon chili jam or
    red pepper jelly

2 tablespoons toasted
    sesame seeds

seasonal salad, to serve

1 Halve the eggplant lengthwise and place skin side up in a large non-stick Dutch oven with ½ inch of boiling water, cover and boil for 10 minutes.

2 Place the rice, shredded coconut and a pinch of sea salt in a saucepan with 1¼ cups of boiling water. Add half the lime, then cover and cook over a medium heat for 12 minutes, or until the rice is tender and the water has been absorbed.

3 Uncover the eggplant, let any excess water cook away, then add 1 tablespoon of olive oil and let it start to fry and crisp up for a few minutes.

4 Mix the miso, soy, honey, rice wine vinegar and chili jam to make a glaze. Flip the eggplant, drizzle with the glaze, and let it fry skin side down on a low heat for 3 minutes to get crispy. Transfer to plates and fold the eggplant pieces in half, sprinkling the flesh side with the sesame seeds and spooning over any remaining glaze from the saucepan.

5 Fluff up the rice and divide alongside, discarding the lime. Serve with a nice delicate salad and fresh lime wedges, for squeezing over.

ENERGY	FAT	SAT FAT	PROTEIN	CARBS	SUGARS	SALT	FIBER
549kcal	17.2g	5.9g	12g	93.6g	20.7g	1.8g	9.3g

SIMPLY PERFECT CHICKEN

USE THIS RELIABLE TECHNIQUE FOR COLOR, JUICINESS & BANG-ON SEASONING – IT WILL ALWAYS DELIVER

SERVES 1
13 MINUTES

1 clove of garlic

1 x 5-oz skinless chicken breast

1 knob of unsalted butter

a few sprigs of thyme

½ a lemon

1 Put a non-stick frying pan on a medium-high heat and, once hot, add a thin layer of olive oil, then squash and add the unpeeled garlic clove.

2 Season the chicken breast all over with sea salt and black pepper and, once the garlic starts to sizzle, lay the chicken into the frying pan, turning every minute for 4 minutes.

3 Add the butter and thyme sprigs, then turn down the heat slightly and cook for 1 more minute on each side, or until perfectly cooked through, angling the frying pan and spooning over the flavored fat.

4 Transfer to a plate to rest for 2 minutes, allowing the juices to travel back to where they should be. Spoon over just a little fat from the frying pan and add a squeeze of lemon juice.

5 Slice the chicken in half at an angle, transfer to a serving plate, then pour over the resting juices and serve with a lemon wedge, for squeezing over, as well as your favorite sides.

ENERGY	FAT	SAT FAT	PROTEIN	CARBS	SUGARS	SALT	FIBER
289kcal	15.4g	6.7g	36.1g	1.4g	0.4g	1.2g	0.5g

SWEET CHILI CHICKEN

SERVES 2 | 10 MINUTES

Finely score **2 x 5-oz skinless chicken breasts** in a crisscross fashion at ½-inch intervals, ½-inch deep. Season with sea salt and black pepper, then place in a non-stick frying pan on a medium-high heat with a thin layer of olive oil and **1 small knob of unsalted butter**. Turn every minute for 6 minutes, or until perfectly cooked through, spooning over the flavored fat. Turn the heat off, drain the fat away, then turn the chicken in **2 tablespoons of sweet chili sauce**. Rest for 2 minutes, then trim and finely slice **2 scallions** and scatter over with **1 teaspoon of black sesame seeds**.

ENERGY	FAT	SAT FAT	PROTEIN	CARBS	SUGARS	SALT	FIBER
280kcal	10.2g	3.9g	36.5g	10.5g	9.5g	1.4g	0.5g

SWEET PEA CHICKEN

SERVES 2 | 10 MINUTES

Blanch **⅔ cup of frozen peas**, then drain. In a mortar and pestle, bash **½ a peeled clove of garlic** with a pinch of sea salt, **2 tablespoons of blanched almonds**, the leaves from **1 bunch of mint (1 oz)** and **3 tablespoons of finely grated Parmesan cheese**. Mix in 1 tablespoon of extra virgin olive oil and the juice of **1 lemon**, season to perfection and gently smash in the peas. Bash **2 x 5-oz skinless chicken breasts** to ½-inch thick. Place in a non-stick frying pan on a high heat with 1 tablespoon of olive oil, turning every minute for 5 minutes, or until perfectly cooked through. Rest for 2 minutes. Serve with the peas and **lemon wedges**.

ENERGY	FAT	SAT FAT	PROTEIN	CARBS	SUGARS	SALT	FIBER
441kcal	25.5g	5.4g	45.5g	7.6g	1.8g	0.9g	2.5g

SPICED CASHEW CHICKEN

SERVES 2 | 10 MINUTES

Slice **2 x 5-oz skinless chicken breasts** into fingers, keeping them intact at the top. Season with sea salt, black pepper and **2 teaspoons of curry powder**. Place in a non-stick frying pan on a medium-high heat with a thin layer of olive oil. Turn every minute for 4 minutes, then add **1 small knob of unsalted butter** and **3 tablespoons of unsalted cashews**. Cook for 2 more minutes, or until perfectly cooked through, spooning over the flavored fat. Divide **3 tablespoons of plain yogurt** between 2 plates, add an extra pinch of curry powder, then the chicken and cashews. Pick over **2 sprigs of cilantro**.

ENERGY	FAT	SAT FAT	PROTEIN	CARBS	SUGARS	SALT	FIBER
341kcal	17.8g	5.9g	40g	5.2g	2.3g	0.8g	0.9g

OLIVE GREMOLATA CHICKEN

SERVES 1 | 10 MINUTES

Finely score **1 x 5-oz skinless chicken breast** at ½-inch intervals, ½-inch deep, then season with sea salt. Place in a non-stick frying pan on a medium-high heat with a thin layer of olive oil, **1 small knob of unsalted butter** and **1 squashed unpeeled garlic clove**. Turn every minute for 6 minutes, or until perfectly cooked through, spooning over the flavored fat. Finely grate the zest of **½ a lemon** onto a board, pick over **2 sprigs of Italian parsley**, add **4 black olives, pitted**, and **½ a red chili**, then very finely chop it all with the garlic and a little lemon juice. Toss with the chicken, rest for 2 minutes and serve.

ENERGY	FAT	SAT FAT	PROTEIN	CARBS	SUGARS	SALT	FIBER
308kcal	17.3g	6.9g	36.6g	1.8g	1.1g	1.3g	0.5g

SPEEDY MICROWAVE GNOCCHI

MAKING HANDMADE GNOCCHI FOR TWO LIKE THIS IS SURPRISINGLY EASY & GIVES MANY SERVING POSSIBILITIES

SERVES 2

18 MINUTES

1 lb russet potatoes

⅓ cup all-purpose flour

PARMESAN SAUCE

1 knob of unsalted butter

1½ oz Parmesan cheese, plus extra to serve

1 whole nutmeg, for grating

1 Prick the potatoes, microwave on full power for 12 minutes, or until soft, then cut in half and use a potato masher to squash out the fluffy middle, putting the skins aside (I keep the skins and fry them in a little olive oil, sea salt and black pepper until crispy – delicious).

2 Mash the fluffy insides, season to perfection with salt and pepper, then lightly mash in the flour. Knead until smooth and pliable, divide in half and roll into 2 long sausage shapes (roughly ¾-inch thick), then slice into 1¼-inch pieces to make your gnocchi – like you see in the pictures.

3 Cook the gnocchi in a saucepan of boiling salted water for 2 minutes, then either add to your chosen sauce (pages 70 to 73) or follow step 4 below.

4 Melt the butter in a non-stick frying pan on a medium heat, then, when the gnocchi is cooked, use a slotted spoon to carefully transfer it into the frying pan, adding a splash of cooking water, if needed. Finely grate in the Parmesan, gently toss until you have a silky, creamy sauce, then serve right away with a fine grating of nutmeg, to taste, and a little extra Parmesan.

ENERGY	FAT	SAT FAT	PROTEIN	CARBS	SUGARS	SALT	FIBER
472kcal	21.8g	10.3g	14.2g	59.1g	2g	0.9g	3.9g

GNOCCHI CARBONARA

SERVES 2 | 6 MINUTES

Slice **4 slices of smoked pancetta** and place in a non-stick frying pan with a little olive oil and a generous pinch of black pepper. In a small bowl, beat **1 egg** with ⅓ **cup of finely grated Parmesan or pecorino cheese**. When the pancetta is golden, turn off the heat and use a slotted spoon to carefully add the **cooked gnocchi** (page 68), gently tossing to coat, then thin the egg mixture with a splash of starchy cooking water. After 1½ minutes, when the frying pan has cooled a little, stir in the egg mixture and agitate together to create a soft, silky sauce, thinning with cooking water, if needed.

ENERGY	FAT	SAT FAT	PROTEIN	CARBS	SUGARS	SALT	FIBER
449kcal	16.8g	6g	23g	59g	2g	1.6g	3.9g

SPICY SALAMI
& TOMATO GNOCCHI

SERVES 2 | 13 MINUTES

Put a non-stick frying pan on a medium heat with 1 tablespoon of olive oil, then add **1½ oz of salami** in one layer, turning when crispy. Remove to a plate, then peel and finely chop **1 clove of garlic** and stir into the tasty fat with **1 pinch of dried red chili flakes** for 30 seconds. Add a **splash of red wine**, cook most of it away, then add **1 x 14-oz can of plum tomatoes**, breaking them up with a potato masher. Simmer for 5 minutes, or until thickened. Season with black pepper, then use a slotted spoon to carefully add the **cooked gnocchi** (page 68), gently tossing to coat. Break over the salami, to finish.

ENERGY	FAT	SAT FAT	PROTEIN	CARBS	SUGARS	SALT	FIBER
473kcal	15.4g	3.9g	13.4g	66g	7.8g	1.5g	5.6g

ZUCCHINI, PEA & MINT GNOCCHI

SERVES 2 | **20 MINUTES**

Peel **1 clove of garlic**, finely slice with **1 zucchini**, then place in a non-stick frying pan on a medium heat with 1 tablespoon of olive oil and **1 pinch of dried red chili flakes** and stir regularly for 10 minutes, or until softened. Strip in most of the leaves from **½ a bunch of mint (½ oz)**, add **½ cup of frozen peas**, cook for 5 minutes, then blitz in a blender with **2 tablespoons of crème fraîche** and **½ oz of Parmesan cheese**. Season to perfection, then pour back into the frying pan and use a slotted spoon to carefully add the **cooked gnocchi** (page 68), gently tossing to coat. Pick over the remaining mint.

ENERGY	FAT	SAT FAT	PROTEIN	CARBS	SUGARS	SALT	FIBER
454kcal	15.3g	6g	16.1g	68.3g	3.3g	0.7g	7.1g

CREAMY GARLIC MUSHROOM GNOCCHI

SERVES 2 | 6 MINUTES

Chop **7 oz of mixed mushrooms**, peel and finely chop **2 cloves of garlic**, then place in a non-stick frying pan with 1 tablespoon of olive oil, and strip in the leaves from **4 sprigs of thyme**. Add a scant ½ cup of water, let it boil down, then fry until lightly golden. Remove from the heat and stir in **2 tablespoons of crème fraîche** and splashes of starchy cooking water until you have a silky sauce. Leave chunky or blitz in a blender, then season to perfection with black pepper and **2 tablespoons of finely grated Parmesan cheese**. Use a slotted spoon to carefully add the **cooked gnocchi** (page 68), gently tossing to coat.

ENERGY	FAT	SAT FAT	PROTEIN	CARBS	SUGARS	SALT	FIBER
410kcal	14.8g	5.8g	12.2g	60.8g	2.6g	0.7g	5.2g

STEAK & NOODLES

BEFORE COOKING SIRLOIN STEAK, FRY IT ON THE FAT SIDE UNTIL GOLDEN & CRISPY TO GAIN BIG BONUS FLAVOR

SERVES 2
22 MINUTES

1 clove of garlic

¾-inch piece of ginger

½ a fresh red chili

2 teaspoons reduced-sodium
    soy sauce

2 tablespoons crunchy
    peanut & sesame chili oil
    (see tip, page 112)

½ a bunch of cilantro (½ oz)

11 oz mixed green veg, such as
    broccolini, asparagus,
    sugar snap peas

1 x 7-oz sirloin steak

2 nests of egg noodles
    (3½ oz total)

2 eggs

2 teaspoons toasted
    sesame seeds

1 Peel the garlic and ginger and finely grate into a large bowl, along with the chili. Add the soy and chili oil and mix well, then tear in most of the cilantro. Trim the veg, halving any thicker broccolini stalks, and set aside.

2 Score the steak fat at ¾-inch intervals, season all over with sea salt and black pepper, then balance the steak fat-side down in a cold non-stick frying pan and place on a high heat to melt and render the fat as the frying pan heats up. Once the fat is golden and crisp, flip the steak onto one of its sides and cook to your liking, turning every minute, then remove to a board to rest – I do 2 minutes on each side for medium-rare.

3 Cook the noodles according to the package instructions, throwing the veg into the water for the last 2 minutes, so they retain their color and crunch. Fry the eggs to your liking in the steak pan, spooning over any tasty fat.

4 Drain the veg and noodles, add to the bowl of dressing, toss to coat and divide between your plates, then sprinkle over the toasted sesame seeds. Slice and add the steaks, spooning over any resting juices, top with the fried eggs, and serve sprinkled with the rest of the cilantro leaves.

ENERGY	FAT	SAT FAT	PROTEIN	CARBS	SUGARS	SALT	FIBER
539kcal	18.1g	4.4g	48.6g	46.4g	5.5g	1.7g	7.7g

GOLDEN PORK & CREAMY PEPPER SAUCE

QUICK COOKING HELPS TO KEEP PORK TENDERLOIN JUICY & TENDER, & THIS SAUCE MAKES IT SOMETHING SPECIAL

SERVES 4

24 MINUTES

1 large onion

1 clove of garlic

1 bunch of sage (¾ oz)

1 x 16-oz jar of roasted
red peppers

1½ cups basmati rice

1 x 1-lb piece of pork
tenderloin

1 level teaspoon smoked
paprika, plus extra
for dusting

⅔ cup sour cream,
plus extra to serve

1 heaping teaspoon
grainy mustard

1 lemon

1 Peel and finely slice the onion and garlic. Put a large non-stick frying pan on a medium-high heat with 2 tablespoons of olive oil, pick in the sage, fry until crispy, then remove to a plate.

2 Add the onion and garlic to the sage oil and fry for 5 minutes, stirring regularly and adding an extra drizzle of oil, if needed, then add the peppers, juice and all, and 1 tablespoon of red wine vinegar.

3 Put the rice into a saucepan with a pinch of sea salt and 2½ cups of boiling water, then cover and cook on a medium-high heat for 12 minutes, or until fluffy and the water has been absorbed. Once done, set aside with the lid on.

4 Cut the pork into four equal-sized pieces. Place a piece of pork between two sheets of parchment paper and use a rolling pin to bash and flatten to ¼-inch thick, then repeat. Season with salt, black pepper and a little paprika.

5 Carefully pour the contents of the frying pan into a blender, add the sour cream, mustard and paprika, blitz until smooth, then season to perfection.

6 Wipe out the frying pan and return to a high heat with 1 tablespoon of oil. Fry the pork for 2 minutes on each side, or until golden and cooked through, working in batches, if needed.

7 Fluff up the rice, and serve with the sauce, pork, crispy sage and lemon wedges, for squeezing over. Finish with an extra pinch of paprika.

ENERGY	FAT	SAT FAT	PROTEIN	CARBS	SUGARS	SALT	FIBER
645kcal	25.3g	8.9g	36.2g	71.8g	7g	1.3g	2.9g

STEAK & MUSHROOM SAUCE

PUSH THE BOAT OUT & TREAT YOURSELF & A LOVED ONE TO A LOVELY FANCY DINNER WITH THIS FAILSAFE RECIPE

SERVES 2
25 MINUTES
PLUS RESTING

1 lb baby potatoes

2 x 5-oz center-cut tenderloin
   steaks, ideally ¾-inch thick

2 sprigs of rosemary

2 knobs of unsalted butter

5 oz mixed mushrooms

2 cloves of garlic

1 heaping teaspoon
   grainy mustard

3 tablespoons brandy

scant ½ cup heavy cream

1½ oz watercress

1 Cook the potatoes in a saucepan of boiling salted water for 15 minutes, or until tender. Once done, drain and leave to steam dry.

2 Place a non-stick frying pan on a high heat and, once hot, add a thin layer of olive oil. Season the steaks with sea salt and black pepper, then cook for 2 minutes on each side for medium-rare, basting regularly, stripping in the rosemary and adding a knob of butter for the final minute. Remove to a plate with the crispy rosemary, pour over some of the pan juices and let rest.

3 Wipe out the frying pan, then tear in the mushrooms and dry-fry for 3 minutes while you peel and finely slice the garlic, then add to the frying pan with a splash of oil and fry for 1 minute, or until lightly golden.

4 Stir through the mustard, pour in the brandy, then carefully tilt the frying pan to catch the flame (or light with a long match) and carefully flambé. When the flames subside, turn off the heat, pour in the cream and leave for 30 seconds to simmer in the residual heat.

5 Toss the potatoes with the remaining knob of butter, season and divide between plates. Spoon the sauce alongside, then slice up and add the steaks, drizzling with the resting juices, and finish with the watercress, dressed simply in a little red wine vinegar, extra virgin olive oil and seasoning.

ENERGY	FAT	SAT FAT	PROTEIN	CARBS	SUGARS	SALT	FIBER
663kcal	33.4g	17.7g	39.7g	39.3g	4.8g	1.2g	3.3g

SMASH BURGER

WHEN ONLY A BURGER WILL DO, THIS SMASH-&-COOK METHOD WILL HAVE YOU COVERED FOR A FAST FILTHY FIX

SERVES 1

12 MINUTES

¼ of a small onion

4½ oz ground beef

1 teaspoon Cajun seasoning

1 burger bun

ketchup

2 pickles

yellow mustard, to serve

1 tomato

1 handful of mixed salad leaves

1 Peel the onion, very finely slice into rounds, then break into rings and cook in a large non-stick frying pan with 1 tablespoon of olive oil for a few minutes, stirring regularly, then push to one side of the frying pan.

2 Squash the ground meat into a rough patty about ¼-inch thick and a bit bigger than your bun and place in the frying pan. Season with black pepper and the Cajun seasoning, then move the onion rings on top and use a slotted spatula to really smash the onions into the meat.

3 Cook for 2 minutes on each side, or until dark, caramelized and cooked through, toasting the halved bun alongside for a minute.

4 Spread the bun base with ketchup, sit the burger on top, slice and layer over 1 pickle, squeeze over mustard to your liking, and pop the lid on.

5 Slice the tomato and remaining pickle to serve on the side with the salad leaves, or stuff it all into your bun, the choice is yours.

ENERGY	FAT	SAT FAT	PROTEIN	CARBS	SUGARS	SALT	FIBER
579kcal	33.3g	10.3g	32.6g	37.3g	12.6g	1.2g	4.2g

WEEKEND
WINS

Invest a little time on a Saturday or Sunday in a largely effortless hero recipe. In return, you'll be graced with nutritious, delicious leftovers, giving multiple easy mealtime options in the inevitably busy days that follow. I cook these up every weekend, without fail.

MY WEEKLY
POACHED
CHICKEN

Poached chicken is the easiest thing to put together, and it's become part of my family's weekend routine. You can get it going on the stove super-quickly and almost forget about it. I never know what I'm going to make in the days that follow, but having cooked chicken and broth ready to go is so, so useful and, of course, you can always enjoy some on the day, too – the choice is yours. Getting ahead like this should save you time and money (as you're investing in the whole chicken for multiple meals), and – the exciting bit – you can take it anywhere you want to on the flavor front. I've shared some of my favorite meals in the pages that follow, but feel free to think up your own, too. The cooked meat and broth will sit happily in your fridge for up to 3 days.

SIMPLE POACHED CHICKEN

THIS IS THE GIFT THAT KEEPS ON GIVING – A HANDS-OFF METHOD THAT MAKES FOR EASY FUTURE MEALS

SERVES 6
(APPROX 1¼ LBS MEAT / 12 CUPS BROTH)

PREP 15 MINUTES

COOK 1 HOUR 30 MINUTES

1 x 3-lb whole chicken

4 carrots

4 stalks of celery

4 cloves of garlic

1 large onion

1 bunch of woody herbs (1 oz),
    such as rosemary, thyme,
    bay leaves, oregano

1 Sit the whole chicken in a large snug-fitting lidded saucepan.

2 Wash, trim and add the carrots. Trim, roughly chop and add the celery, along with the unpeeled garlic cloves. Peel, quarter and add the onion. Add the herbs with 2 teaspoons of sea salt and 1 teaspoon of black peppercorns.

3 Cover everything with cold water, making sure the bird is fully submerged, then bring nearly to a boil over a high heat and immediately turn down to a gentle simmer. Cover with a lid ajar and poach for 1½ hours, then you can either eat it straight away, or leave it to cool in the broth ready to break down for the week ahead.

4 Pour the broth into a jug. Remove the chicken skin to a small bowl, then strip all the meat off the bones and into a container. Discard the bones. Spoon over any fat from the surface of the broth onto the meat, then toss together. Reserve the veg in a separate container, squeezing the garlic out of the skins. Cover, and it'll all be happy in the fridge for up 3 days – the hard work is done. It might not look that pretty but, rest assured, this preparation gives so much flex for big flavor and super-fast meals.

LEFTOVER LOVE

Even if I lived alone, I'd cook this. If you're worried about not using it all up in time, just portion up and whack the different elements in the freezer, where they'll keep happily for up to 3 months. Simply thaw thoroughly before use.

ENERGY	FAT	SAT FAT	PROTEIN	CARBS	SUGARS	SALT	FIBER
277kcal	9.8g	2.8g	38.6g	9g	5.6g	0.9g	3.2g

INDIAN-INSPIRED STREET FOOD SALAD

IF YOU'VE NEVER TRIED A SALAD LIKE THIS YOU'RE MISSING OUT – VIVACIOUS, VIBRANT & UTTERLY DELICIOUS

SERVES 2
23 MINUTES

6 tablespoons plain yogurt

1 tablespoon unsweetened shredded coconut

1 mixed bunch of mint & cilantro (1 oz)

1 lime

5 oz shredded poached chicken (page 86)

1½ oz Bombay mix

1½ oz puffed rice cereal

½ a pomegranate

1 lb mixed crunchy veg, such as English cucumber, tomatoes, carrots, cauliflower

2 tablespoons jarred pickled red cabbage

½ teaspoon curry powder

1 Make a dressing by blitzing the yogurt, coconut, most of the herb leaves and the lime juice in a blender until smooth, then season to perfection with sea salt and black pepper, adding a splash of water to thin, if needed.

2 Divide the shredded chicken between two serving bowls with the Bombay mix and puffed rice. Hold the pomegranate half cut side down in the palm of your hand and tap with the back of a spoon so all the seeds tumble out through your fingers into the bowls.

3 Prep and delicately shred, grate, slice, chop or peel your chosen crunchy veg so it's all a pleasure to eat. Divide between the bowls, along with the pickled cabbage.

4 Pick over the remaining herb leaves, dust over the curry powder, then add the dressing, toss well and tuck in.

ENERGY	FAT	SAT FAT	PROTEIN	CARBS	SUGARS	SALT	FIBER
460kcal	18.1g	5.9g	32.1g	43.1g	15.2g	1.2g	7g

CHICKEN NOODLE BROTH

IN JUST 10 MINUTES YOU CAN BE SLURPING ON THIS SATISFYING, WARMING, TASTY BOWL OF DELICIOUSNESS

SERVES 1
10 MINUTES

2½ oz thick rice noodles

1¼ cups chicken broth
    (page 86)

1–2 tablespoons crunchy
    peanut & sesame chili oil
    (see tip, page 112)

2 scallions

2 sprigs of cilantro

3½ oz shredded poached
    chicken (page 86)

3½ oz crunchy veg, such as
    carrots, sugar snap peas,
    snowpeas, baby corn

reduced-sodium soy sauce

½ a lime

1 Cook the noodles according to the package instructions, then drain and transfer to a warm serving bowl.

2 Return the empty noodle pan to the heat, pour in the broth and bring to a boil, while you dress the noodles with the chili oil, to taste. Finely shred the scallions and pile on top of the noodles with the cilantro leaves.

3 Drop the chicken and crunchy veg into the broth (halving any baby corn lengthwise, and using a vegetable peeler to strip in the carrot, if using) for 2 minutes, or until the chicken is hot through.

4 Taste the broth, season to perfection with a little soy, then spoon over the noodles with the chicken and veg. Add a good squeeze of lime juice, some extra chili oil, if you like a real kick, and tuck in.

ENERGY	FAT	SAT FAT	PROTEIN	CARBS	SUGARS	SALT	FIBER
571kcal	12.5g	2.7g	39.4g	72.8g	7.9g	1g	3.8g

CREAMY CHICKEN & CHIVE PIE

FUN & FAST TO ASSEMBLE, & IMPRESSIVE LOOKING WITHOUT THE FUSS, I KNOW THIS PIE WILL SERVE YOU WELL

SERVES 6
PREP 10 MINUTES
COOK 35 MINUTES

1 lb shredded poached chicken
 & veg (page 86)

1 bunch of chives (¾ oz)

1 cup sour cream

2 tablespoons reduced-fat milk

2 tablespoons grainy mustard

2 x 11-oz sheets of ready-
 rolled puff pastry (cold)

1 egg

2 tablespoons sesame seeds

1 Preheat the oven to 400°F. Roughly chop the poached veg and place in a bowl with the shredded chicken. Finely slice and add the chives, along with the sour cream, milk, mustard and a pinch of sea salt and black pepper, then mix well.

2 Unroll one of the pastry sheets, leaving it on its paper, place it on a baking sheet, trim it to size, if needed, then spoon and flatten the pie filling across the center, leaving a 1¼-inch border all the way around the edge.

3 Beat the egg and brush the exposed pastry. Unroll the second sheet of pastry over the top, remove the top sheet of paper, then use a fork to seal the pastry edges together and brush the top with eggwash.

4 Sprinkle over the sesame seeds, cut a little cross in the center, then place the baking sheet over a medium heat on the stove for just 1 minute, to start crisping up the base – no one likes a soggy bottom.

5 Bake on the bottom rack of the oven for 30 minutes, or until golden and cooked through. Amazing served with a mixed salad or some steamed seasonal veg.

ENERGY	FAT	SAT FAT	PROTEIN	CARBS	SUGARS	SALT	FIBER
608kcal	39.6g	19.3g	20.9g	62.6g	4.4g	1.6g	3.1g

CHICKEN, LEEK & POTATO SOUP

FALL BACK IN LOVE WITH HOMEMADE SOUP WITH THIS FRESH FOWL TAKE ON THE CLASSIC LEEK & POTATO COMBO

SERVES 4

35 MINUTES

1¾ oz leftover chicken skin (page 86)

3½ slices of bread (3½ oz total)

1 bunch of Italian parsley (1 oz)

1 lb leeks

1 lb potatoes

optional: 5 oz poached chicken veg (page 86)

5 cups chicken broth (page 86)

5 oz shredded poached chicken (page 86)

5 tablespoons sour cream

4 teaspoons jarred horseradish

1 Finely slice any leftover chicken skin and fry until lightly golden in a large deep saucepan on a medium-high heat with 1 tablespoon of olive oil. Cube and add the bread (removing the crusts), toss until golden, tearing in 2 sprigs of parsley for a final minute, then remove, leaving the saucepan on the heat.

2 Trim the leeks, halve lengthwise and wash, then finely slice and place in the saucepan with a splash of water or broth. Peel the potatoes and chop into small chunks, adding them to the saucepan as you go, then chop and add any poached veg, if using. Cook for 15 minutes, or until softened, stirring occasionally and adding splashes of water, if needed.

3 Cover with 4 cups of broth and bring to a boil, then add the chicken and simmer for 5 minutes.

4 In batches, blitz the soup in a blender with the sour cream until smooth, thinning with the extra broth, if needed, then season to perfection and divide three-quarters of the soup between serving bowls.

5 Blitz the remainder of the soup with the rest of the parsley and the horseradish, stirring that vivid green through the creamy soup in your bowls.

6 Pile on the crispy chicken skin and parsley croutons, add a pinch of black pepper, drizzle with a little extra virgin olive oil, if you like, and serve.

ENERGY	FAT	SAT FAT	PROTEIN	CARBS	SUGARS	SALT	FIBER
421kcal	17.9g	5.6g	27.8g	38.2g	0.8g	0.8g	2.4g

EASY CHICKEN FLATBREAD

IT ALWAYS SURPRISES ME HOW QUICKLY YOU CAN CRISP UP TENDER COOKED CHICKEN TO CREATE AN EPIC BITE

SERVES 1

10 MINUTES

2½ oz shredded poached chicken (page 86)

1 tablespoon sesame seeds

1 flatbread

1 heaping tablespoon hummus

¼ of a little gem lettuce

2½-inch piece of English cucumber

2 sprigs of Italian parsley

1 teaspoon liquid honey

¾ oz feta cheese

1 tablespoon pomegranate seeds

½ a lemon

1 Place the chicken (and a few strips of leftover chicken skin, if you've got it) in a non-stick frying pan on a high heat with ½ a tablespoon of olive oil and a pinch of sea salt and black pepper. Let it crisp up and get golden for 3 minutes, adding the sesame seeds for the last minute while you warm the flatbread through by placing it on top.

2 Remove the flatbread to a plate. Spread the hummus across the flatbread, then shred the lettuce, matchstick the cucumber, and tear up the parsley leaves, piling them on top.

3 Drizzle the honey over the chicken and toss to coat, then scatter it over the flatbread, crumble over the feta, and sprinkle with the pomegranate seeds.

4 Finish with a little extra virgin olive oil, season to perfection, and add squeezes of lemon juice, to taste. Roll, wrap and enjoy!

ENERGY	FAT	SAT FAT	PROTEIN	CARBS	SUGARS	SALT	FIBER
481kcal	25.5g	6g	34.3g	27.5g	5.1g	1.2g	3.9g

SPEEDY CHICKEN CURRY

SOMETIMES ONLY A CURRY WILL DO – THIS ONE COMES TOGETHER VERY QUICKLY & IS JAM-PACKED WITH FLAVOR

SERVES 4

20 MINUTES

1 red onion

1½ cups basmati rice

2 tablespoons chili & garlic curry paste or your favorite curry paste

1 tablespoon mango chutney

10½ oz shredded poached chicken (page 86)

1 x 15-oz can of chickpeas

11 oz frozen leaf spinach

11 oz ripe mixed-color tomatoes

1 x 13½-oz can reduced-fat coconut milk

optional: ½ a bunch of cilantro (½ oz)

1 Peel and finely chop the onion and place in a frying pan on a medium-high heat with 1 tablespoon of olive oil, stirring regularly for 5 minutes.

2 Put the rice into a saucepan with 2½ cups of boiling water or reserved chicken broth (page 86) and a small pinch of sea salt, cover and cook on a medium-high heat for 12 minutes, or until all the liquid has been absorbed.

3 Stir the curry paste and mango chutney into the onion pan for 2 minutes, then go in with the chicken, drained chickpeas, frozen spinach and tomatoes, halving or quartering any larger ones. Cook for 5 minutes, stirring regularly.

4 Pour in the coconut milk and simmer vigorously for 5 minutes, or until the sauce is reduced to the consistency that you like, the spinach has thawed and the rice is done. Season the curry to perfection with salt and black pepper, serve with the rice, and pick over the cilantro, if using.

ENERGY	FAT	SAT FAT	PROTEIN	CARBS	SUGARS	SALT	FIBER
596kcal	14.9g	7.1g	36.4g	82.9g	9.3g	0.8g	5.5g

CHICKEN, SAUSAGE & MUSHROOM STEW

IN THE TIME THE RICE COOKS YOU CAN HAVE THIS OUTRAGEOUSLY DELICIOUS, DELICATE LITTLE NUMBER READY

SERVES 2

19 MINUTES

¾ cup basmati rice

1 pork sausage

5½ oz mixed mushrooms

1 onion

4 sprigs of thyme

2 teaspoons English mustard

scant ½ cup heavy cream

5 oz shredded poached chicken
(page 86)

3½ oz baby spinach

cayenne pepper

1 Put the rice into a saucepan with 1¼ cups of boiling water or reserved chicken broth (page 86) and a small pinch of sea salt, cover and cook on a medium-high heat for 12 minutes, or until all the liquid has been absorbed.

2 Squeeze the sausagemeat out of the skin, breaking it into little balls, then place in a frying pan on a medium-high heat and fry for 3 minutes.

3 Tear in the mushrooms, peel, very finely slice and add the onion, strip in the thyme, add ½ a tablespoon of olive oil and fry for 5 minutes, or until softened and lightly golden, stirring regularly.

4 Stir in the mustard, cream and ⅔ cup of water or reserved broth, followed by the chicken and spinach. Turn down to a simmer for 5 minutes, then season the stew to perfection with salt and black pepper. Serve with the rice and a pinch of cayenne pepper, to taste.

ENERGY	FAT	SAT FAT	PROTEIN	CARBS	SUGARS	SALT	FIBER
866kcal	39g	14g	43.9g	90.8g	8.7g	1.6g	4.6g

CHICKEN OPEN SANDWICH

SERVES 1 | 5 MINUTES

Toast **1 slice of whole wheat bread**. Peel and finely slice **½ a ripe avocado**. Dress the avo and **1 small handful of watercress** with a good squeeze of **lemon juice** and a little extra virgin olive oil, and season to perfection. Lay the avo on the toast. Mix **2½ oz of shredded poached chicken** (page 86) with **1 tablespoon of mayonnaise**, a good squeeze of **lemon juice** and **4 chopped sprigs of tarragon leaves**, then season to perfection. Pile on top, add the watercress, and finish with a sprinkling of **mixed seeds**.

ENERGY	FAT	SAT FAT	PROTEIN	CARBS	SUGARS	SALT	FIBER
476kcal	32.1g	5g	25.2g	21.4g	4.6g	1g	3.9g

CHICKEN BUN

SERVES 1 | 5 MINUTES

Mix **2½ oz of shredded poached chicken** (page 86) with **1 tablespoon of mayonnaise**, **1 heaping teaspoon of sun-dried tomato paste** and **1 chopped sprig of basil leaves**, then season to perfection with sea salt and black pepper. Pile into a **bread bun** of your choice, with some sliced **ripe tomato**, **1 small handful of your favorite lettuce leaves**, a little crumbling of **goat cheese**, and a couple of extra basil leaves. Finish with a pinch of black pepper.

ENERGY	FAT	SAT FAT	PROTEIN	CARBS	SUGARS	SALT	FIBER
507kcal	25.4g	5.6g	28.9g	40.9g	11.2g	1.7g	4.5g

BATCH-IT-UP BOLOGNESE

Taking care of and investing time in a wonderful Bolognese as it cooks, enjoying some for dinner, then benefiting from that care for months to come by bagging it and freezing it, is, to me, a no-brainer. And the recipes I've shared that help you utilize that freezer stash go well beyond spag Bol – these are exciting lunches and dinners that will make you feel satisfied in no time at all.

A BETTER BOLOGNESE

A HEALTHIER RAGÙ OF GROUND BEEF, PORK & LENTILS THAT YOU CAN BATCH UP & USE IN A MULTITUDE OF FUTURE MEALS

SERVES 14
PREP 40 MINUTES
COOK 2 HOURS

2 sprigs of rosemary

4 slices of smoked bacon

9 oz ground beef

9 oz ground pork

2 onions

2 carrots

2 cloves of garlic

2 stalks of celery

1 lb mixed mushrooms

⅔ cup tomato paste

2 tablespoons balsamic vinegar

3 x 14-oz cans of lentils
(or 1½ cups cooked lentils)

3 x 14-oz cans of plum
tomatoes

1 lb baby back ribs

1 Pick and finely chop the rosemary leaves, finely slice the bacon, then place in a large deep Dutch oven on a high heat with ¼ cup of olive oil, stirring regularly, until lightly golden.

2 Add all the ground beef and pork, breaking it up with your spoon, and let it brown for 15 minutes, stirring regularly.

3 Peel the onions, carrots, garlic and celery and finely chop with the mushrooms (I pulse it all in a food processor to save time), then add to the Dutch oven and cook for another 15 minutes, stirring regularly.

4 Stir in the tomato paste and balsamic, then tip in the lentils, juice and all. Add the tomatoes, then fill each can with water, swirl around and pour into the Dutch oven.

5 Bring to a boil, then halve and add the rack of ribs. Simmer on a medium-low heat for 2 hours, mashing occasionally with a potato masher to thicken the texture, and scraping up all the nice sticky bits from the bottom of the Dutch oven.

6 Season to perfection with sea salt and black pepper, remove the rib bones, then portion up what you need, stashing the rest in the fridge (for up to 3 days) or freezer (for up to 3 months), ready for future meals.

VEGGIE LOVE

Simply swap the bacon, ground meat and ribs for 1 lb of veggie ground meat substitute, skipping steps 2 and 5 and adding the veggie substitute at step 4.

ENERGY	FAT	SAT FAT	PROTEIN	CARBS	SUGARS	SALT	FIBER
225kcal	11.6g	3.6g	17g	14.2g	5.2g	0.2g	1.6g

PESTO GNOCCHI BOLOGNESE BAKE

ASSEMBLY DINNERS ARE SO HELPFUL – THIS PAN OF FAMILY FAVORITE INGREDIENTS IS A SURE WIN

SERVES 4
28 MINUTES

3½ cups A better Bolognese
(page 106)

11 oz frozen leaf spinach

2 tablespoons pesto,
plus extra to serve

1 lb potato gnocchi

1 x 4½-oz ball of
mozzarella cheese

1½ oz Parmesan cheese

1 Preheat the broiler to high. Put the Bolognese into a 9 x 13-inch roasting pan with the spinach and heat over a medium heat on the stove for about 10 minutes, or until bubbling and the spinach has thawed, stirring occasionally and thinning with splashes of water, if needed.

2 Stir through the pesto, scatter over the gnocchi, tear over the mozzarella, finely grate over the Parmesan, and drizzle with 1 tablespoon of olive oil.

3 Place the pan under the broiler for 12 minutes, or until golden and bubbling, then serve with a few extra bombs of pesto, if you fancy, and a sprinkling of black pepper. Dinner, done.

ENERGY	FAT	SAT FAT	PROTEIN	CARBS	SUGARS	SALT	FIBER
598kcal	30g	11.4g	36.5g	46.8g	8g	1.5g	4.3g

BOLOGNESE STUFFED PEPPERS

IT'S SO EASY TO FILL PEPPERS WITH BOLOGNESE, YET THE FINISHED RESULT LOOKS & TASTES JUST SUBLIME

SERVES 4

33 MINUTES

4 peppers

1⅔ cups A better Bolognese
(page 106)

1 heaping tablespoon
harissa paste

1¾ oz Manchego cheese

7 oz ripe mixed-color cherry
tomatoes

8 mixed-color olives (with pits)

½ a bunch of Italian parsley
(½ oz)

chili sauce, to serve

1 Preheat the broiler to high. Halve the peppers through the stalks and seed, then rub with a little olive oil, sea salt and black pepper and sit them in a snug-fitting roasting pan, cut side down. Broil for 5 minutes, then flip the peppers over and broil for another 5 minutes.

2 Reheat the Bolognese in a saucepan on a medium heat, stirring occasionally and adding splashes of water to thin, if needed, then stir in the harissa.

3 Divide the Bolognese into the peppers, slice and lay over the cheese, and place back under the broiler for a final 3 to 5 minutes, or until golden.

4 Quarter the tomatoes, pit and tear up the olives, pick the parsley leaves, and toss it all with a little extra virgin olive oil, red wine vinegar, salt and pepper. Scatter this fresh salsa over the peppers, and serve with a drizzle of chili sauce, to taste. Nice with bread to mop up the tasty juices.

AIR-FRYER IT

Prep the peppers as per step 1, then cook in an air fryer at 400°F for 10 minutes, in batches if needed, flipping halfway. Continue until the peppers are filled in step 3, then cook in the air fryer for 3 to 5 minutes, or until golden.

ENERGY	FAT	SAT FAT	PROTEIN	CARBS	SUGARS	SALT	FIBER
273kcal	15.8g	5.4g	15.9g	18.1g	12.4g	1.2g	5.6g

SPICY BOL & BLACK BEAN NOODLES

JUST A COUPLE OF EXTRA INGREDIENTS TOTALLY TRANSFORM THIS BOLOGNESE INTO A SPICY, WARMING DELIGHT

SERVES 2

19 MINUTES

1 cup A better Bolognese
(page 106)

1 x 15-oz can of black beans

2 tablespoons crunchy peanut
& sesame chili oil,
plus extra to serve

11 oz mixed green veg, such as
broccolini, asparagus, baby
bok choy, snowpeas

5 oz thick rice noodles

sesame oil

1 Put the Bolognese, black beans, juice and all, and chili oil into a small saucepan on a medium heat and reheat until bubbling, stirring occasionally and adding splashes of water to thin to a soupy consistency.

2 Quarter any baby bok choy lengthwise, and halve any thicker broccolini stalks. Cook the noodles according to the package instructions, either steaming the veg above in a colander with a lid on or blanching them separately.

3 Drain the noodles, divide between two serving bowls with the veg and toss with a little sesame oil, then spoon the spicy Bolognese into the bowls, drizzle with a little extra chili oil, if you like, and serve.

INGREDIENT LOVE

It's worth hunting out a really good chili oil with chunky bits of peanut and sesame seeds, and ideally some garlic, because it delivers so big on flavor and has the power to totally transform your Bolognese, and more!

ENERGY	FAT	SAT FAT	PROTEIN	CARBS	SUGARS	SALT	FIBER
480kcal	16.4g	4g	32.3g	44.6g	8.6g	0.6g	20.9g

HALLOUMI, PEA & BOL SAMOSAS

CRISP, CRUNCHY PASTRY IS THE PERFECT VESSEL FOR BOLOGNESE SPIKED WITH SPICE & PEAS – HAPPY DAYS

SERVES 2
PREP 18 MINUTES
COOK 25 MINUTES

¾ cup A better Bolognese
(page 106)

1 cup frozen peas

1 tablespoon tikka masala
curry paste

1¾ oz halloumi cheese

3 sheets of phyllo pastry

1 little gem lettuce

3 sprigs of cilantro

½ an English cucumber

1 tablespoon pomegranate
seeds

1 Preheat the oven to 400°F. Put the Bolognese into a bowl with the peas and curry paste, then grate in the halloumi and mix well.

2 Lay out the pastry sheets and cut them in half. Working fairly quickly, divide the filling into six, placing it in one corner of each sheet, then fold the pastry over a few times to create a triangle shape and wrap the filling, brushing the pastry with olive oil as you go.

3 Place the samosas on an oil-rubbed baking sheet, brush the tops with a little oil, and bake for 25 minutes, or until golden and crisp.

4 Prep your salad – separate the lettuce leaves, pick the cilantro leaves, and cut up the cucumber. Add the pomegranate seeds, dress it all with a little extra virgin olive oil, red wine vinegar, sea salt and black pepper, and serve with the hot samosas.

AIR-FRYER IT

Brush the samosas with oil and cook in a single layer in an air fryer at 400°F, in batches if needed, for 10 minutes, or until golden and crisp.

ENERGY	FAT	SAT FAT	PROTEIN	CARBS	SUGARS	SALT	FIBER
536kcal	33.2g	8.8g	27.7g	47.2g	10.5g	1.6g	9.6g

BAKED BOLOGNESE CRÊPES

TAKE TWO FAMILY BIG HITTERS, BOLOGNESE & CRÊPES, ADD SOME OOZY CHEESE, HEAT IT UP & YOU'RE AWAY

SERVES 4

PREP 26 MINUTES

COOK 25 MINUTES

1 large egg

1¾ cups whole wheat flour

1⅓ cups of milk

2 cups A better Bolognese (page 106)

3 oz Cheddar cheese

½ x 16-oz jar of roasted red peppers

½ a bunch of fresh basil (½ oz)

1 Preheat the oven to 350°F. To make the crêpe batter, whisk the egg into the flour with a pinch of sea salt, then whisk in the milk until smooth.

2 Put a 12-inch non-stick ovenproof frying pan on a medium heat. Once hot, add a drizzle of olive oil and swirl one quarter of the batter around the frying pan. Cook for 2 to 3 minutes, or until lightly golden on both sides, remove and repeat, laying the crêpes on a clean work surface as you go.

3 Spoon a quarter of the Bolognese across one half of each crêpe, then crumble or grate over the cheese. Drain, roughly slice and add the peppers, tear over most of the basil leaves, then fold each crêpe into quarters and place back in the frying pan (like you see in the picture).

4 Bake for 25 minutes, or until golden and crisp. Serve sprinkled with the remaining basil leaves. Nice with a salad.

ENERGY	FAT	SAT FAT	PROTEIN	CARBS	SUGARS	SALT	FIBER
448kcal	19.5g	8.3g	27.8g	43.3g	8.8g	5.6g	1.2g

CHEESY BOLOGNESE BUNS

SOMETIMES THE SIMPLE THINGS IN LIFE ARE THE BEST, LIKE THESE NAUGHTY TOASTY CHEESY BOLOGNESE BUNS

SERVES 4

16 MINUTES

2 cups A better Bolognese
(page 106)

4 crusty bread buns

2 cloves of garlic

4 sprigs of thyme

3½ oz Camembert cheese

1 Preheat the oven to 350°F. Reheat the Bolognese in a saucepan on a medium heat, stirring occasionally and thinning with a little water, if needed.

2 Slice the tops off the buns and set aside, then use a small knife to help you hollow out the soft bun middles. Peel and halve the garlic cloves, rub the cut sides around the inside of each bun, then sit the buns in a roasting pan, tear the soft middles around them, and sit the bun lids alongside them.

3 Finely slice the garlic and throw into the roasting pan, in and around the buns, strip in the thyme leaves, then drizzle with 1 tablespoon of olive oil. Add a quarter of the cheese to each bun and bake for 10 minutes, or until the cheese has melted and the buns are golden.

4 Load the Bolognese into each bun and pop the lids on, using the crispy bits as croutons and to mop up any excess Bolognese.

AIR-FRYER IT ————————————

Prep as directed above, stripping the thyme leaves into the garlic-rubbed buns before you add the cheese. Place the buns, soft middles and garlic in an air fryer at 350°F in a single layer, in batches if needed. Drizzle with 1 tablespoon of olive oil and cook for 4 minutes, then load with Bolognese.

ENERGY	FAT	SAT FAT	PROTEIN	CARBS	SUGARS	SALT	FIBER
429kcal	18.6g	7g	23.3g	44.9g	5.8g	1.1g	3.3g

VERSATILE CORNBREAD

Easy to knock together and oh-so satisfying, this recipe brings me so much joy. A whole cornbread, fresh from the oven, sitting proudly in the middle of the table, seems to always make people happy. And not only that, you can use it in so many cool and contemporary ways. You'll have fun with this one!

EASIEST CORNBREAD

THIS CHUCK-IT-ALL-IN METHOD, WHERE YOU CAN BAKE & SERVE IN THE PAN, MEANS LESS FUSS BUT BIG FLAVOR

SERVES 12+
PREP 11 MINUTES
COOK 30 MINUTES

1 x 11-oz can of corn

⅔ x 12-oz jar of sliced
jalapeños

1¼ cups of cottage cheese

scant ½ cup reduced-fat milk

2 cups yellow cornmeal

2¾ cups self-rising flour

1 heaping teaspoon
baking powder

4 large eggs

1 bunch of scallions

3½ oz Cheddar cheese

1 Preheat the oven to 400°F. Tip the corn and jalapeños (with the juice from both) into a large bowl with the cottage cheese, milk, cornmeal, flour and baking powder, then crack in the eggs.

2 Trim, finely slice and add the scallions, chop and add most of the Cheddar, along with 6 tablespoons of olive oil, then season well with sea salt and black pepper and give it all a good mix together.

3 Transfer the mixture into a 12-inch non-stick ovenproof frying pan, spread it out evenly and smooth the top, crumble over the remaining Cheddar, drizzle with a little more oil, then bake for 30 minutes, or until risen and golden.

4 Enjoy it warm, fresh from the oven, or cool, wrap and store in the fridge for up to 3 days, ready for future meals.

ENERGY	FAT	SAT FAT	PROTEIN	CARBS	SUGARS	SALT	FIBER
267kcal	13.3g	4.3g	10.3g	28.6g	2.1g	1.2g	1.6g

DIPPY EGGS & CORNBREAD SOLDIERS

5 MINUTES

Lightly toast **fingers of cornbread** (page 122) in a non-stick frying pan on a medium heat or in an air fryer at 375°F for 8 minutes, turning until golden on all sides, then serve with **soft-boiled eggs** for dunking. I like to add **a slice or two of smoked bacon** to the frying pan (or the air fryer for the last 5 minutes) for extra flavor.

CREAM CHEESE MARMITE & AVO

5 MINUTES

Toast a **slice of cornbread** (page 122) in a non-stick frying pan on a medium heat until lightly golden on both sides, then spread with **cream cheese**, add some delicate cubes of **lime-dressed seasoned ripe avocado**, and drizzle with a little extra virgin olive oil and with **Marmite**, to taste.

HAM, SLAW & MUSTARD

5 MINUTES

Serve a **wedge of freshly baked cornbread** (page 122), or warm through in a frying pan or the oven, with **smoked ham**, **English mustard** and a **seeded slaw**. I like to finely shred or peel mixed crunchy veg and fruit like **cabbage**, **carrot**, **apple** and **pear**, then toss with **mayonnaise**, **yogurt**, a little (too much) **mustard** of your choice, extra virgin olive oil and red wine vinegar. Season to perfection and toss with **mixed seeds**.

EGGY CORNBREAD

8 MINUTES, PLUS SOAKING

Soak **sliced cornbread** (page 122) in seasoned **beaten eggs** for 15 minutes, turning the cornbread halfway. Once the time's up, char **ripe tomatoes** in a frying pan on a medium heat until beautifully golden, adding the cornbread to cook on both sides for the last couple of minutes. Serve with **lime-dressed ripe avocado** and a crumbling of **walnuts**, a few **fresh mint leaves** and a little drizzle of extra virgin olive oil.

FUSS-FREE CAULIFLOWER CHEESE

CRUMBLED CORNBREAD PROVIDES THE ULTIMATE IN SUPER-SATISFYING FLAVOR-PACKED CRISPY TOPPINGS HERE

SERVES 4–6 AS A SIDE
PREP 10 MINUTES
COOK 50 MINUTES

1 head of cauliflower (1¾ lbs)

1¼ cups heavy cream

1 teaspoon English mustard

3½ oz Cheddar cheese

3½ oz Easiest cornbread
(page 122)

1 Preheat the oven to 350°F. Remove and discard just the tatty outer leaves from the cauliflower, then break it apart into 1½-inch florets, finely slice the stalk, and place it all in a 9 x 13-inch roasting pan in a single layer.

2 Toss with 1 tablespoon of olive oil and a pinch of sea salt and black pepper, roast for 40 minutes, then remove the pan from the oven and carefully squash the cauliflower with a fork to break it up a bit.

3 Mix the cream and mustard together, season, then pour evenly over the cauliflower. Finely grate over the cheese, crumble over the cornbread and bake for a final 10 minutes, or until golden and bubbling.

ENERGY	FAT	SAT FAT	PROTEIN	CARBS	SUGARS	SALT	FIBER
399kcal	30.1g	16.1g	16.3g	16.9g	8g	0.9g	4g

SMOKY CORNBREAD OMELET

6 MINUTES

Chop up **smoked bacon** and fry with **cubes of cornbread** (page 122) in a non-stick frying pan on a medium heat until golden, then tip out. Beat some **eggs**, season and pour into the frying pan, swirling to cover the base. Scatter the crispy cornbread and bacon back on top, tear over a little **melty cheese, like Camembert or Brie**, pop a lid on the frying pan and turn down to a low heat until cooked through. Nice with a **tomato salad** on the side.

FRENCH-STYLE SALAD

5 MINUTES

Toast **little chunks of cornbread** (page 122) in a frying pan on a medium heat until golden, toasting **a few mixed seeds** alongside. Make a quick **French dressing** (page 43), then use to dress your favorite **salad leaves**. Spoon over the crispy cornbread and seeds, and enjoy.

PASTA ALFREDO

TOASTED CORNBREAD MAKES THE BEST CRISPY SPRINKLE, ESPECIALLY WHEN SCATTERED OVER SILKY PASTA SAUCES

SERVES 2

16 MINUTES

5 oz dried fettuccine
  or tagliatelle

1 slice of Easiest cornbread
  (page 122)

2 cloves of garlic

1 small knob of unsalted butter

⅔ cup heavy cream

1 oz Parmesan cheese,
  plus extra to serve

1 Cook the pasta according to the package instructions.

2 Crumble the cornbread into a frying pan on a medium heat with a drizzle of olive oil and toast until golden, tossing regularly, then remove to a small bowl, leaving the frying pan on the heat.

3 Peel and very finely slice the garlic, place in the hot pan with 1 tablespoon of oil and the butter and cook for 2 minutes, or until soft but not colored.

4 Pour in the cream, add a ladle of starchy pasta water, and let it simmer until reduced to a loose silky sauce consistency.

5 Use tongs to transfer the pasta straight into the sauce, then – off the heat – finely grate and stir in the Parmesan, season to perfection with sea salt and black pepper, and stir until silky and decadent, thinning with a little extra cooking water, if needed.

6 Scatter over or mix through the crispy crumbs and serve, adding an extra grating of Parmesan to finish, if you like.

ENERGY	FAT	SAT FAT	PROTEIN	CARBS	SUGARS	SALT	FIBER
729kcal	40.9g	18.3g	22.5g	72.5g	5.4g	1g	3g

MOZZARELLA
& CHARRED VEG

6 MINUTES

Snap the woody ends off some **asparagus**, then cook it in a hot grill pan with a **vine of ripe cherry tomatoes** until bar-marked, adding a **wedge of cornbread** (page 122) to lightly char on both sides for the last couple of minutes. Alternatively, cook all three in a single layer in an air fryer at 375°F for 8 minutes, spritzing the asparagus and tomatoes with oil and turning the cornbread halfway. Serve with torn **mozzarella**, a drizzle of extra virgin olive oil, a squeeze of **lemon juice** and a pinch of sea salt and black pepper.

MANGO & FETA CORNBREAD SALAD

5 MINUTES

Char **thin slices of cornbread** (page 122) in a hot grill pan until bar-marked, while you chop **English cucumber**, **radishes**, **ripe mango** and **feta cheese** into similar-sized chunks, and dress with **lime juice**, extra virgin olive oil and a little sea salt and black pepper. Tear over the charred cornbread, add **fresh mint** and **basil leaves**, toss well, and serve.

CORNBREAD CRUMBED SHRIMP

WHETHER COATING SHRIMP, STRIPS OF FISH OR CHICKEN, CORNBREAD CRUMBS WILL ROCK YOUR FLAVOR WORLD

SERVES 2
14 MINUTES

5½ oz raw peeled jumbo shrimp

3½ tablespoons all-purpose flour

1 egg

4½ oz stale Easiest cornbread (page 122)

½ a lemon

6 tablespoons plain yogurt

1 tablespoon sriracha chili sauce

1 little gem lettuce

1 Run a small sharp knife down the back of each shrimp to butterfly it, also removing the vein, then dust each shrimp with flour.

2 Beat the egg in a shallow bowl. Blitz the cornbread into crumbs, then tip onto a plate. Toss the flour-dusted shrimp in the beaten egg (letting the excess drip off), then coat in the cornbread crumbs.

3 Put a large non-stick frying pan on a medium-high heat and, once hot, add a thin layer of olive oil. Cook the shrimp for 3 minutes, or until golden and cooked through, turning regularly.

4 On a platter, mix the lemon juice into the yogurt, season with a pinch of sea salt and spread out across the platter, then erratically ripple through the sriracha and a few drips of extra virgin olive oil.

5 Separate out the lettuce leaves and serve it all together, dunking as you go. Add flatbreads on the side to turn it into more of a meal, if you like.

LEFTOVER LOVE

Any stale cornbread (page 122) can be blitzed into crumbs — fine or chunky, the choice is yours — and stashed in the freezer for up to 3 months, to add extra flavor to all sorts of meals.

ENERGY	FAT	SAT FAT	PROTEIN	CARBS	SUGARS	SALT	FIBER
422kcal	24.3g	5.9g	26g	26.4g	5.2g	1.6g	2.4g

THE
SAUCE
WE ALL NEED

I find that in my house, we're often in need of a base tomato sauce for a whole myriad of different meals. And, in my mind, if you're going to make a sauce, why not make one packed with a whole rainbow of veggies, meaning you can get more of the good stuff into your friends and family, maybe without them even knowing! What follows is a bunch of recipes that celebrate this sauce in diverse ways, from a simple soup to a proper fancy dinner.

SECRET VEG SAUCE

GET MORE VEG IN YOUR LIFE! THIS TASTY SAUCE CAN BE USED IN SO MANY WAYS, IT'S A GREAT FREEZER STAPLE

**MAKES 16–20 CUPS,
20 PORTIONS
1 HOUR 30 MINUTES**

2 red onions

2 carrots

2 small bulbs of fennel

½ a head of celery

2 red bell peppers

½ a butternut squash (1¼ lbs)

1 teaspoon dried rosemary

3 x 14-oz cans of plum
    tomatoes

1 Preheat the oven to 425°F. Peel the onions, wash and trim the carrots, fennel and celery, seed the peppers and squash (there's no need to peel it), then roughly chop it all.

2 Place the veg in a large high-sided roasting pan, and toss with 2 tablespoons of olive oil, the dried rosemary and a pinch of sea salt and black pepper.

3 Cover tightly with aluminum foil and roast for 30 minutes, then remove the foil and roast for a further 30 minutes, or until soft and caramelized.

4 In three batches, blitz one third of the veg with one can of tomatoes and half a can of water (swirl it around the can), then season to perfection – whether you go super-smooth or a little bit chunky is up to you.

5 Divide between reusable bags or containers, and pop in the fridge for up to 3 days, or freeze for up to 3 months. Tasty meals await!

ENERGY	FAT	SAT FAT	PROTEIN	CARBS	SUGARS	SALT	FIBER
58kcal	1.5g	0.2g	1.8g	10g	5.3g	0.2g	3.2g

CREAMY TOMATO SOUP

SERVES 2 | 10 MINUTES

Put **2 cups of Secret veg sauce** (page 140) into a saucepan with ¾ cup of water, place over a medium heat until hot through, then swirl in **¼ cup of heavy cream** and season to perfection with sea salt and black pepper. While it heats, toast **2 slices of bread or 4 slices of French baguette**, then spread with **2 tablespoons of your favorite pesto**. Serve sprinkled with a few fresh basil leaves, if you've got them.

ENERGY	FAT	SAT FAT	PROTEIN	CARBS	SUGARS	SALT	FIBER
358kcal	14g	4.9g	10.6g	48.6g	13.3g	1.1g	8.3g

EMERGENCY KIDS' PIZZA

SERVES 1 | 9 MINUTES

Place **1 small flatbread or flour tortilla** on a baking sheet and spread with **2 tablespoons of Secret veg sauce** (page 140), then tear over **¼ x 4½-oz ball of mozzarella**. Have fun with minimal toppings – **finely sliced veg, olives and antipasti, leftover roast chicken, canned fish or capers** will all serve you well. Grate over a little **Parmesan cheese**, and place under the broiler until the cheese has melted.

ENERGY	FAT	SAT FAT	PROTEIN	CARBS	SUGARS	SALT	FIBER
293kcal	11.1g	6g	12.4g	34.2g	6.3g	1.2g	6.6g

CHICKEN EGGPLANT MILANESE

MILANESE IS AN ITALIAN CLASSIC & BY TEAMING CHICKEN WITH EGGPLANT, YOU GET DOUBLE THE PLEASURE

SERVES 2

25 MINUTES

1 x 5-oz skinless chicken breast

1 eggplant (9 oz)

1 egg

1⅓ cups panko breadcrumbs

2 tablespoons all-purpose flour

5 oz dried spaghetti

1 cup Secret veg sauce
   (page 140)

½ x 4½-oz ball of mozzarella

2 sprigs of basil

½ a lemon

1 Very carefully slice through the chicken breast, giving you two flat pieces. Cover with a sheet of parchment paper, bash with a rolling pin to tenderize and flatten to ½-inch thick, then season with sea salt and black pepper. Slice four ¼-inch-thick rounds of eggplant (saving the rest for another day).

2 Beat the egg in a shallow bowl. Scatter the breadcrumbs into another. Dust the chicken and eggplant slices with flour, turn them in the egg, letting any excess drip off, then evenly coat with the breadcrumbs.

3 Cook the spaghetti according to the package instructions. At the same time, pour ½ inch of olive oil into a large non-stick frying pan on a medium-high heat and, once hot, cook the chicken and eggplant for 3 to 4 minutes on each side, or until golden and cooked through, then remove to paper towels.

4 Drain the pasta, reserving a cupful of starchy cooking water. Quickly reheat the Secret veg sauce in the empty pan, tossing the pasta back through it. Thin with a splash of cooking water, if needed, and season to perfection.

5 Serve with the crispy chicken and eggplant slices, topped with torn-up mozzarella and basil leaves, with lemon wedges, for squeezing over.

AIR-FRYER IT

Spritz the breaded chicken and eggplant with oil and cook in a single layer in an air fryer at 400°F, in batches if needed, for 10 minutes, or until golden and cooked through, turning and spritzing with oil halfway.

ENERGY	FAT	SAT FAT	PROTEIN	CARBS	SUGARS	SALT	FIBER
801kcal	28.1g	8.1g	43.5g	99.1g	11.5g	1.6g	6.2g

EASY BAKED BEANS

SERVES 2 | 9 MINUTES

Pour **1 x 15-oz can of cannellini beans** (also known as white kidney beans), juice and all, into a frying pan on a medium heat with 1 tablespoon of olive oil and **1 cup of Secret veg sauce** (page 140). Simmer for 5 minutes, or until you have a nice consistency, season to perfection with sea salt and black pepper, then spoon over hot **buttered toast**. Grate over **1 oz of Red Leicester or your favorite English Cheddar cheese**, and finish with a dash of **Worcestershire sauce or a drizzle of Marmite**.

ENERGY	FAT	SAT FAT	PROTEIN	CARBS	SUGARS	SALT	FIBER
369kcal	14.7g	4.7g	16.4g	39.3g	6.2g	0.9g	11.4g

QUICK CODDLED EGGS

SERVES 2 | 10 MINUTES

Put a large non-stick frying pan on a medium heat with **1 cup of Secret veg sauce** (page 140), 1 tablespoon of olive oil and **3½ oz of baby spinach**. Crack **4 eggs** onto the spinach, slice and lay over **1¾ oz of goat cheese**, sprinkle with a little sea salt and black pepper, then cover and cook for 3 to 5 minutes, or until the eggs are cooked to your liking. Serve with warm hunks of **crusty bread**, for dipping and dunking.

ENERGY	FAT	SAT FAT	PROTEIN	CARBS	SUGARS	SALT	FIBER
270kcal	18.1g	6.7g	18.7g	9.7g	5.6g	1.2g	2.6g

FRAGRANT SPICY FISH SOUP

I LOVE MUSSELS, AS THEY'RE SO QUICK TO COOK & WORK SO WELL WITH THESE SWEET AROMATIC FLAVORS

SERVES 2

13 MINUTES

1 lb mussels, scrubbed,
    debearded

5 oz fillet of white fish,
    skin on, pin-boned

4 raw shell-on extra jumbo
    shrimp

½–1 fresh red chili

4 sprigs of cilantro

1 heaping tablespoon of
    your favorite curry paste

1 cup Secret veg sauce
    (page 140)

½ x 13½-oz can of reduced-fat
    coconut milk

1 lime

1 Check the mussels – tap any open ones, and if they don't close, discard them. Slice the fish lengthwise into four equal pieces. Peel the shells off the shrimp, leaving the heads and tails intact, then run the tip of your knife down the back of each one and remove the vein. Finely slice the chili and pick the cilantro leaves.

2 Put a large deep pan on a high heat with 1 tablespoon of olive oil and the curry paste, cook for 1 minute, then stir in the Secret veg sauce, coconut milk and mussels. Lay the fish over the mussels, top with the shrimp, then season with a small pinch of sea salt, finely grate over half the lime zest and squeeze over half the juice. Scatter in the chili.

3 Cover and bring to a boil for 4 minutes, or until the fish and shrimp are just cooked through and all the mussels have opened and are soft and juicy. If any remain closed, discard them.

4 Sprinkle over the cilantro leaves, and serve with lime wedges, for squeezing over. Nice with shrimp chips or pappadams, for dunking.

ENERGY	FAT	SAT FAT	PROTEIN	CARBS	SUGARS	SALT	FIBER
324kcal	15.1g	6g	33g	14.7g	6.8g	1.8g	3.8g

ONE-PAN DINNERS

Colorful and flavor-packed, you can't beat the satisfaction of these delicious assembly meals, where after an initial few minutes of getting everything together, the oven does all the hard work for you. Weeknight or weekend, that's dinner, sorted.

ROASTED VEG WITH CAMEMBERT FONDUE

EVERYTHING TASTES BETTER WITH OOZY MELTED CHEESE, & HERE, HUMBLE VEG SING AFTER A GENTLE ROAST

SERVES 6
PREP 7 MINUTES
COOK 55 MINUTES

3 sweet potatoes (1¾ lbs total)

3 mixed-color bell peppers

3 cloves of garlic

3 mixed-color onions

9 oz Camembert cheese

1 French baguette

½ a bunch of basil (½ oz)

1 Preheat the oven to 400°F. Scrub the sweet potatoes and slice into ½-inch-thick rounds. Seed the peppers and slice into chunky wedges. Peel and slice the garlic. Toss it all in a large roasting pan with 1 tablespoon each of olive oil and red wine vinegar and a pinch of sea salt and black pepper.

2 Halve the unpeeled onions and carefully place cut side down directly on the oven rack, placing the roasting pan of veg beneath. Roast for 45 minutes.

3 Remove the roasting pan from the oven and use tongs to move the onions to your board, then remove the skins, break the onions apart and toss with the veg.

4 Leaving a ½-inch rim around the edge, cut the rind off the top of the Camembert, then nestle it into the middle of the roasting pan, drizzle with a little oil, season with black pepper and bake for a final 10 minutes, warming the baguette alongside. Pick over the basil leaves, and serve!

ENERGY	FAT	SAT FAT	PROTEIN	CARBS	SUGARS	SALT	FIBER
475kcal	11.7g	6g	18.3g	74.2g	16g	1.7g	9.8g

GOLDEN MISO SALMON

GOING HARD & FAST WITH THE BROILER ADDS AN EXTRA DIMENSION OF FLAVOR, CREATING A SATISFYING MEAL

SERVES 4
23 MINUTES

1 lb asparagus

11 oz sugar snap peas

1 tablespoon dark miso

2 tablespoons reduced-sodium soy sauce

1 tablespoon sesame oil

2 limes

4 x 5-oz salmon fillets, skin on, scaled, pin-boned

1 tablespoon sesame seeds

1 carrot

2 scallions

4 radishes

4 sprigs of fresh mint

1 Preheat the broiler to high. Snap the woody ends off the asparagus and place it in a 9 x 13-inch roasting pan with the sugar snap peas, then drizzle with 1 tablespoon of olive oil and shake to coat.

2 Mix the miso, soy and sesame oil in a shallow bowl, then finely grate in the zest of 1 lime and squeeze in the juice to make a marinade. Slice the salmon fillets in half lengthwise, toss in the marinade, then drape over the veg in the roasting pan, drizzling over the excess marinade. Scatter over the sesame seeds.

3 Broil for 12 minutes, or until the greens are blistered and the salmon is golden and just cooked through.

4 To make a quick pickle, peel and matchstick the carrot, trim and finely chop the scallions, finely slice the radishes, pick and roughly chop the mint leaves, then dress it all with lime juice, sea salt and black pepper.

5 Scatter the pickle over the salmon in the roasting pan, and serve. Delicious with noodles or fluffy rice on the side.

ENERGY	FAT	SAT FAT	PROTEIN	CARBS	SUGARS	SALT	FIBER
396kcal	24.2g	3.9g	36.3g	8.6g	5.8g	1.3g	3.4g

SICHUAN PEPPER BEEF BRISKET

FULL OF PUNCHY FLAVORS, THIS EASY HANDS-OFF METHOD WILL GIVE YOU TENDER MEAT & A FUN-FILLED MEAL

SERVES 6

PREP 18 MINUTES

COOK 3 HOURS

2 large red onions

2 oranges

4 cloves of garlic

1½-inch piece of ginger

2 tablespoons reduced-sodium soy sauce

2 tablespoons balsamic vinegar

2 tablespoons liquid honey

4 teaspoons Sichuan peppercorns

2 lbs brisket, unrolled

4 teaspoons Chinese 5-spice powder

1 English cucumber

6 nests of vermicelli rice noodles (10½ oz total)

½ a bunch of cilantro (½ oz)

2 tablespoons toasted sesame seeds

1 Preheat the oven to 275°F. Peel and roughly chop the onions, place in a small high-sided roasting pan, then halve the oranges and squeeze in the juice. Peel, finely chop and scatter in the garlic and ginger, then drizzle in the soy, balsamic and honey and mix together.

2 Grind the Sichuan peppercorns in a mortar and pestle until fine, then rub all over the meat with the Chinese 5-spice powder, a pinch of sea salt and black pepper and a little olive oil. Sit the meat on top of the onions, cover tightly with aluminum foil, and roast for 3 hours, or until tender and pullable, adding splashes of water occasionally to prevent it from drying out, if needed.

3 Finely slice the cucumber into rounds, then toss with a pinch of salt and 2 tablespoons of red wine vinegar. Rehydrate the noodles according to the package instructions, then drain well.

4 Remove the roasting pan from the oven and discard the foil, then use forks to break the meat apart, tossing it back through the onions and tasty pan juices. Serve with the noodles, cucumber, cilantro leaves and toasted sesame seeds, and let everyone help themselves. Nice with sprouts or delicate seasonal leaves in the mix, too.

EASY SWAPS

If you can't get your hands on Sichuan peppercorns, you could use 4 teaspoons of Sichuan chili oil instead, just omit the olive oil when you're rubbing the spices onto the meat.

ENERGY	FAT	SAT FAT	PROTEIN	CARBS	SUGARS	SALT	FIBER
704kcal	31.2g	11.8g	36.6g	68.3g	15.2g	1.4g	1.2g

GARLIC MUSHROOM CODDLED EGGS

CELEBRATING EARTHY MUSHROOMS, SPUDS & SPINACH, THIS EASY ONE-PAN DISH IS A PLEASURE TO MAKE & EAT

SERVES 4
PREP 12 MINUTES
COOK 30 MINUTES

1 lb mixed mushrooms

3½ oz baby spinach

4 cloves of garlic

1 lb potatoes

4 eggs

8 baby cornichons or 2 pickles

2½ oz soft goat cheese

1 Preheat the oven to 400°F. Tear or roughly chop the mushrooms, chop the spinach, then put it all into a 9 x 13-inch roasting pan, peel and finely grate in the garlic, add 2 tablespoons of olive oil and a pinch of sea salt and black pepper and toss well.

2 Scrub the potatoes, slice as finely as you can, rub with 2 tablespoons of oil, season, then layer over the veg. Roast for 25 minutes, or until lightly golden.

3 Remove the pan from the oven and mix everything together, then make four little wells and crack in the eggs. Return to the oven for a final 5 minutes, or until the eggs are coddled to your liking.

4 Finely slice and scatter over the cornichons or pickles, spoon over the goat cheese, drizzle with a little extra virgin olive oil and finish with a pinch of pepper.

ENERGY	FAT	SAT FAT	PROTEIN	CARBS	SUGARS	SALT	FIBER
364kcal	23.8g	6g	14.8g	24.4g	2.6g	1.6g	3.3g

CHIMICHURRI MEATLOAF

GROUND MEAT IS A GREAT CARRIER OF FLAVORS – HERE WE'RE GOING ARGENTINIAN STYLE FOR AN EPIC MEALTIME

SERVES 8
PREP 20 MINUTES
COOK 1 HOUR

1 clove of garlic

1 fresh red chili

1 bunch of Italian parsley (1 oz)

1 bunch of cilantro (1 oz)

2 lbs ground beef & pork

1 large egg

3⅔ cups fresh breadcrumbs

1 x 16-oz jar of roasted
    red peppers

7 oz sliced melty cheese,
    such as Emmental

2 red onions

2 x 15-oz cans of black beans

2 tablespoons liquid honey

1 Preheat the oven to 400°F. To make the chimichurri, peel the garlic and finely chop with the chili, parsley and cilantro leaves. Scrape into a bowl, add 1 tablespoon each of red wine vinegar and extra virgin olive oil, and season to perfection with sea salt and black pepper.

2 In a large bowl, scrunch together the ground meat, egg, breadcrumbs and half the chimichurri, then pat out the mixture to 12 x 15 inches on a large sheet of oil-rubbed parchment paper. Drain the peppers, tear open and lay them evenly over the ground meat, then top with the sliced cheese.

3 Use one of the long sides of the paper to help you roll the ground meat up, patting, pressing and shaping it into a meatloaf, then transfer it to a large high-sided roasting pan and carefully release it, fold side down, discarding the paper.

4 Peel and quarter the onions, add to the roasting pan and drizzle everything with a little olive oil. Cover the pan with aluminum foil and roast for 30 minutes.

5 Pull out the roasting pan, discard the foil and baste the meatloaf with the pan juices. Pour the beans around the loaf, juice and all, along with a swig of vinegar. Drizzle the honey over the loaf and roast for a final 30 minutes.

6 Slice, and serve with the sticky onions and beans, with the remaining chimichurri spooned on top. Great with fluffy rice, mashed potato, sweet potato wedges or crusty hunks of bread.

ENERGY	FAT	SAT FAT	PROTEIN	CARBS	SUGARS	SALT	FIBER
504kcal	26.9g	12.1g	39.6g	23.3g	9.4g	1g	8.1g

SUMMERY SALMON

KNOWING SOMETHING SO COLORFUL & BEAUTIFUL CAN BE ON THE TABLE IN JUST 20 MINUTES IS JOYFUL

SERVES 4

20 MINUTES

1½ x 14½-oz cans of peeled
   new potatoes

4 x 5-oz salmon fillets,
   skin on, pin-boned

1 lb ripe cherry tomatoes
   on the vine

scant ¾ cup black olives, pitted

1 heaping tablespoon capers
   in brine

½ a bunch of oregano (½ oz)

1 lemon

4 slices of prosciutto

4 heaping teaspoons pesto

1 Preheat the broiler to high. Drain the potatoes, place in a 9 x 13-inch roasting pan, toss with 1 tablespoon of olive oil, then place on the stove over a medium heat for 5 minutes, or until the potatoes begin to get golden.

2 In a bowl, mix the salmon, vine tomatoes, olives and capers with the oregano leaves, 1½ tablespoons of oil and juice of half the lemon. Pull out the salmon fillets and wrap in the prosciutto, then pour the contents of the bowl into the roasting pan and sit the salmon on top, skin side down.

3 Broil for 10 minutes, or until golden and the salmon is just cooked through.

4 Dollop over the pesto and serve with lemon wedges, for squeezing over.

EASY SWAPS

Green beans, asparagus and broccolini would all be delicious here. Canned potatoes are brilliant for quick cooking, but you could also swap in store-bought potato gnocchi.

ENERGY	FAT	SAT FAT	PROTEIN	CARBS	SUGARS	SALT	FIBER
500kcal	32.1g	5.4g	35.5g	16.8g	4g	1.8g	2.1g

GARLIC BREAD BEAN & FISH BAKE

A FUN WAY TO ENJOY WHITE FISH, BOOSTED WITH ZESTY LEMON, FRAGRANT ROSEMARY & A BIT OF OVEN LOVE

SERVES 4

27 MINUTES

1 lemon

2 sprigs of rosemary

4 x 5-oz white fish fillets, skin off, pin-boned

2 x 15-oz cans of cannellini beans (also known as white kidney beans)

11 oz ripe cherry tomatoes

4 anchovy fillets in oil

3½ oz garlic bread

1 Preheat the oven to 400°F. Finely grate the zest of 1 lemon onto a board, strip over the rosemary leaves and finely chop, then rub all over the fish fillets with 1 tablespoon of olive oil and a pinch of sea salt and black pepper.

2 Drain the cannellini beans and tip into an 11 x 15-inch roasting pan. Halve the cherry tomatoes and scatter most of them into the roasting pan, then chop and add the anchovy fillets, along with a drizzle of oil from the jar. Squeeze in the juice of ½ a lemon, season with black pepper and toss well.

3 In a blender or food processor, blitz the garlic bread into crumbs, then sprinkle over the beans, sit the dressed fish fillets on top, scatter over the remaining tomatoes and bake for 15 minutes, or until golden and the fish is perfectly cooked through.

4 Serve with a drizzle of extra virgin olive oil, if you like, and lemon wedges, for squeezing over. Great with a crunchy green salad.

ENERGY	FAT	SAT FAT	PROTEIN	CARBS	SUGARS	SALT	FIBER
320kcal	15.3g	3.9g	40g	27.2g	4g	1.1g	9.9g

CHICKEN & MUSHROOM BAKE

AN EASY & COZY PEOPLE-PLEASER THAT USES CANNED SOUP AS A SHORTCUT TO BIG FLAVOR – WE LOVE THAT

SERVES 4

PREP 5 MINUTES

COOK 1 HOUR

4 large chicken thighs,
  skin on, bone in

1 lb mixed mushrooms

1 x 10½-oz can of Campbell's
  condensed mushroom soup

1½ cups basmati rice

1 x 15-oz can of butter beans

1 lemon

7 oz frozen leaf spinach

4 teaspoons English mustard,
  plus extra to serve

1 Preheat the oven to 400°F. In a 9 x 13-inch roasting pan, toss the chicken with 1 tablespoon of olive oil and a pinch of black pepper, then scatter in the mushrooms, tearing any larger ones (if you like your chicken skin extra crispy, fry the thighs until golden before adding the mushrooms).

2 Tip in the soup, then drain and tip in the butter beans, followed by the rice. Fill the bean can with water and pour into the pan. Finely grate in the lemon zest, then mix everything together.

3 Bring the chicken to the top, skin side up, making sure the rice is submerged, then nestle in the frozen spinach. Cover with oiled aluminum foil and bake for 50 minutes, or until the chicken is cooked through and the rice is tender, removing the foil for the last 5 minutes. Fluff up the rice and spinach and season to perfection.

4 Mix the mustard with the lemon juice in a small bowl, then drizzle over the bake, and serve.

EASY SWAPS

Canned mushroom soup provides deep flavor here, but creamy chicken would give good results, too. Other frozen veg, such as cauliflower or green beans, work well in place of the spinach, and you can swap in any canned beans you fancy.

ENERGY	FAT	SAT FAT	PROTEIN	CARBS	SUGARS	SALT	FIBER
644kcal	23.1g	5g	31.1g	77.3g	3g	1.6g	4.1g

ROASTED MED VEG & FETA BAKE

HERO-ING THOSE GENIUS BAGS OF MIXED ROASTED VEG FROM THE FREEZER SAVES BIG ON THE PREP TIME HERE

SERVES 4
PREP 5 MINUTES
COOK 30 MINUTES

1¾ cups couscous

1 x 15-oz can of chickpeas

1½ lbs frozen chargrilled
   Mediterranean veg

1 heaping tablespoon
   harissa paste

7 oz block of feta cheese

1 lemon

1 heaping teaspoon
   dried oregano

1 Preheat the oven to 400°F. Tip the couscous into a 9 x 13-inch roasting pan, then mix in the chickpeas, juice and all.

2 Toss the frozen veg with the harissa and a pinch of sea salt and black pepper, then layer on top of the couscous and chickpeas.

3 Quarter the feta and arrange on top, then halve the lemon, place half in the middle, and squeeze the other half over everything. Sprinkle with the oregano and drizzle with 2 tablespoons of olive oil.

4 Roast for 30 minutes, or until everything's beautifully golden. Fork up the couscous, use tongs to squeeze over the jammy roasted lemon, and serve. Delicious with a seasonal salad on the side.

EASY SWAPS

If you can't get hold of frozen chargrilled Mediterranean veg, simply chop your favorite seasonal veg into ¾-inch chunks instead.

ENERGY	FAT	SAT FAT	PROTEIN	CARBS	SUGARS	SALT	FIBER
538kcal	21.1g	8.4g	21g	69.8g	3.3g	1.4g	6.5g

GOCHUJANG CHICKEN NOODLE BAKE

GOCHUJANG IS A KOREAN CHILI PASTE THAT TAKES THIS HUMBLE CHICKEN DISH UP A SERIOUS NOTCH

SERVES 4
PREP 12 MINUTES
COOK 50 MINUTES

2 x 2½-inch pieces of ginger
　　(3 oz total)

4 cloves of garlic

1 small green cabbage,
　　such as sweetheart

4 large chicken thighs,
　　skin on, bone in

2 heaping tablespoons
　　gochujang paste

4 nests of vermicelli rice
　　noodles (7 oz total)

1 bunch of scallions

2 tablespoons sesame seeds

1 Preheat the oven to 400°F. Peel and finely slice the ginger and garlic, quarter the cabbage lengthwise, then place it all in a 9 x 13-inch roasting pan with the chicken thighs and gochujang paste.

2 Drizzle everything with 1 tablespoon of olive oil and 2 tablespoons of red wine vinegar, add a pinch of black pepper, then mix well, massaging that flavor in. Arrange the chicken skin side up and roast for 30 minutes.

3 Plunge the noodles into a bowl of boiling water for 1 minute, then remove the roasting pan from the oven and use tongs to drag the noodles into the pan, dressing them in the pan juices, and nestling them in the corners. Trim the scallions, finely slice and reserve the green tops, then add the lengths to the roasting pan. Move the chicken thighs to sit back on top – we want the skin to get nice and crispy.

4 Pour ¾ cup of cold water into the roasting pan, scatter over the sesame seeds, then roast for another 20 minutes, or until the chicken is cooked through, the cabbage is tender and the noodles have hydrated in all the cooking juices. Scatter over the reserved scallion tops, to serve.

ENERGY	FAT	SAT FAT	PROTEIN	CARBS	SUGARS	SALT	FIBER
549kcal	23g	5.9g	30.1g	55.4g	8.9g	1.3g	5.4g

CHEAT'S TUNA PASTA BAKE

THIS DISH BREAKS ALL THE RULES, BUT IT'S EASY & ANNOYINGLY DELICIOUS – YOU'LL ENJOY THIS ONE

SERVES 6
PREP 18 MINUTES
COOK 45 MINUTES
PLUS RESTING

2 x 10½-oz cans of Campbell's condensed mushroom soup

10½ oz cremini mushrooms

10½ oz dried pasta shells

2 x 5-oz cans of tuna in water

1 lemon

1 fresh red chili

3 cups arugula

2½ oz Cheddar cheese

1 lb red-skinned potatoes

1 Preheat the oven to 400°F. Tip the soup into a 9 x 13-inch roasting pan, then refill each can with water, swirl around and pour into the pan.

2 Halve or quarter the mushrooms, depending on their size, and add to the pan with the pasta and drained tuna. Finely grate in the lemon zest and squeeze in the juice. Slice and add the chili, roughly chop and add most of the arugula, season with a little sea salt and black pepper, and mix well.

3 Coarsely grate over the cheese, scrub the potatoes and slice as finely as you can, then layer over the top and gently press them down.

4 Drizzle with olive oil and bake for 45 minutes, or until golden and bubbling, then stand for 15 minutes. Scatter over the remaining arugula, and serve.

ENERGY	FAT	SAT FAT	PROTEIN	CARBS	SUGARS	SALT	FIBER
420kcal	13.6g	4g	21.1g	56.2g	2.7g	1.8g	1.6g

MEDITERRANEAN LAMB

MINIMAL INGREDIENTS & A SLOW ROAST CREATE THIS IMPRESSIVE YET TOTALLY EFFORTLESS CROWD-PLEASER

SERVES 8
PREP 12 MINUTES
COOK 5 HOURS

8 onions

2½ lbs potatoes

1 cup green olives, pitted

1 bunch of rosemary (¾ oz)

½ x 2-oz tin of anchovy fillets in oil

¾ cup dry white wine

1 x 4½-lb lamb shoulder, bone in

1 Preheat the oven to 325°F, and boil 4 cups of water.

2 Peel and halve the onions, scrub and halve the potatoes, quartering any larger ones, then place in your largest high-sided roasting pan.

3 Chuck in the olives, strip in the rosemary and drape over the anchovy fillets, then pour in 4 cups of boiling water and the wine.

4 Sit the lamb on top, season all over with sea salt and black pepper, then tightly cover the roasting pan with aluminum foil and carefully transfer to the oven to roast for 4½ hours, or until the lamb is super-tender and melt-in-your-mouth – there's no need to check it, just let the oven do its thing.

5 Remove the foil, baste the lamb well with the juices from the roasting pan and cook for a final 30 minutes, or until golden.

6 Pull off chunks of meat and divide between plates, discarding any bones. Mix up everything in the roasting pan, then plate up the potatoes, onions and olives, along with some of the tasty juices. Serve with seasonal greens or salad.

ENERGY	FAT	SAT FAT	PROTEIN	CARBS	SUGARS	SALT	FIBER
633kcal	36g	15.6g	37.4g	38.6g	10.4g	1.6g	5.2g

GRAPE & COUSCOUS CHICKEN BAKE

SIMPLE TO PUT TOGETHER, ELEGANT & VERY TASTY, IT'S ALWAYS NICE TO TAKE YOUR TASTE BUDS ON A HOLIDAY

SERVES 4

PREP 16 MINUTES

COOK 50 MINUTES

4 large chicken thighs,
   skin on, bone in

1 bunch of thyme (¾ oz)

1 lb red seedless grapes

2 tablespoons Dijon mustard

2 tablespoons sumac, plus
   extra to serve

1 bunch of scallions

1¾ cups couscous

1 x 15-oz can of chickpeas

2 tablespoons shelled unsalted
   pistachios

¼ cup plain yogurt

1 Preheat the oven to 350°F. Place the chicken thighs in a 9 x 13-inch roasting pan, strip in the thyme leaves, and add the grapes, mustard, sumac, 1 tablespoon of olive oil and a pinch of sea salt and black pepper.

2 Trim the scallions, finely slice and reserve the green tops, then add the whole white lengths to the roasting pan. Toss it all together well, sit the chicken thighs on top skin side up, and roast for 30 minutes.

3 Remove the roasting pan from the oven and pour in the couscous and the chickpeas, juice and all. Add a scant ½ cup of water and stir well, picking up all the nice sticky bits, then arrange the chicken back on top, skin side up, and roast for another 20 minutes, or until the chicken is perfectly cooked through.

4 Finely chop the pistachios and sprinkle with the reserved scallion tops, then finish with dollops of yogurt and an extra dusting of sumac.

ENERGY	FAT	SAT FAT	PROTEIN	CARBS	SUGARS	SALT	FIBER
711kcal	23.6g	6g	37.7g	91.5g	23.8g	1.4g	8.8g

SPICY PANEER & VEG SQUASH BAKE

SWEET ROASTED VEG, FRAGRANT CURRY PASTE & CREAMY PANEER TEAM UP IN THIS TASTY VEGGIE NUMBER

SERVES 4

1 HOUR 35 MINUTES

1 butternut squash (2½ lbs)

1 onion

1 eggplant (9 oz)

1 lemon

1 heaping tablespoon chili
   & garlic or your
   favorite curry paste

1½ cups basmati rice

1 bunch of cilantro (1 oz)

2 tablespoons mango chutney

6 oz paneer cheese

1 Preheat the oven to 400°F. Carefully halve the squash lengthwise, seed, then rub with 1 tablespoon of olive oil, sea salt and black pepper and place cut side down directly on the top rack of the oven.

2 Peel and quarter the onion, chop the eggplant into 2-inch chunks and place it all in a 9 x 13-inch roasting pan. Finely grate over the lemon zest, season with salt and pepper, and toss well with the curry paste and a little oil. Sit the roasting pan on the rack beneath the squash and roast for 50 minutes, or until everything is soft, then remove the roasting pan and the squash from the oven.

3 Transfer the onion and eggplant to a board, then sprinkle the rice into the pan. Season, stir in 2½ cups of boiling water, then nestle in half the lemon and place over a high heat on the stove for 3 minutes, or until just boiling.

4 Use a spoon to scoop the squash flesh out onto the board with the onion and eggplant, leaving a ¼-inch layer inside. Sprinkle most of the cilantro leaves over the veg and roughly chop it all together, season to perfection, then spoon it into the squash halves. Nestle them into the rice, spoon over half the mango chutney, then grate over the paneer and carefully return to the oven for 15 minutes.

5 Fluff up the rice, sprinkle with the remaining cilantro, dollop over the rest of the mango chutney and serve with lemon wedges, for squeezing over.

ENERGY	FAT	SAT FAT	PROTEIN	CARBS	SUGARS	SALT	FIBER
580kcal	14g	5.6g	18.3g	100.9g	24g	1.8g	7.6g

WEEKEND PORK SHOULDER

PORK SHOULDER DOES GREAT THINGS GIVEN TIME IN THE OVEN – CRACKLING & TENDER PULLABLE MEAT, JOY

SERVES 6

PREP 10 MINUTES

COOK 4 HOURS

2 teaspoons fennel seeds

4½ lbs pork shoulder,
   bone out

6 baking potatoes

6 onions

6 bay leaves

2 apples

5½ oz watercress

mustard, to serve

1 Preheat the oven to 425°F. Bash the fennel seeds in a mortar and pestle until fine. Sit the pork in a large roasting pan and randomly score the skin all over, rub with olive oil, the fennel, sea salt and black pepper, then roast for 1 hour. Halve the potatoes, and peel and halve the onions.

2 Remove the roasting pan from the oven and baste the pork with the pan juices, then remove it to a plate for a moment. Add the potatoes and onions to the roasting pan and carefully toss with the bay leaves, 2 tablespoons of red wine vinegar, and a pinch of salt and pepper, then sit the pork on top.

3 Return the roasting pan to the oven, turn down the temperature to 325°F and roast for 3 hours, basting the pork and tossing the veg halfway, also adding a splash of water occasionally to prevent it from drying out, if needed.

4 Matchstick the apples, toss with the watercress, a little extra virgin olive oil, a swig of red wine vinegar and seasoning. Shred the pork and onions to your liking, then serve everything with the potatoes and a dollop of your favorite mustard on the side.

ENERGY	FAT	SAT FAT	PROTEIN	CARBS	SUGARS	SALT	FIBER
713kcal	35.8g	11g	43.6g	57g	12.2g	1.1g	5.2g

GNARLY LAMB MADRAS

GET THIS IN THE OVEN IN NO TIME, THEN SIT BACK & ENJOY THE COOKING AROMAS – PERFECT FOOD TO SHARE

SERVES 8

PREP 9 MINUTES

COOK 5 HOURS

1 x 4½-lb lamb shoulder,
  bone in

⅔ x 10-oz jar of Madras
  curry paste

1 heaping cup yellow split peas

4 red onions

1 potato

4 tomatoes

2½-inch piece of ginger

1 bulb of garlic

½ a bunch of cilantro (½ oz)

12 cloves

1 Preheat the oven to 325°F, and boil 5 cups of water.

2 Lightly score the skin side of the lamb all over in a crisscross fashion, then season with sea salt and black pepper and rub with half of the curry paste.

3 Place the yellow split peas in your largest high-sided roasting pan, then peel, halve and add the onions and potato. Halve the tomatoes, peel and chop the ginger, break up the garlic bulb and roughly chop the cilantro (stalks and all), then add everything to the pan, along with the remaining curry paste.

4 Stir in 5 cups of boiling water, then sit the lamb on top, scatter over the cloves, tightly cover the roasting pan with oiled aluminum foil and carefully transfer to the oven to roast for 4½ hours, or until the lamb is super-tender and melt-in-your-mouth – there's no need to check it, just let the oven do its thing.

5 Remove the foil, baste the lamb well with the juices from the roasting pan, and cook for a final 30 minutes, or until golden, dark and caramelized.

6 Pull off chunks of meat and divide between serving plates, discarding any bones. Break up the potato, squeeze out the soft garlic and stir both through the split peas and veg, then plate up, along with some of the tasty juices.

ENERGY	FAT	SAT FAT	PROTEIN	CARBS	SUGARS	SALT	FIBER
633kcal	36g	15.6g	37.4g	38.6g	10.4g	1.6g	5.2g

CHICKEN IN BAKED BREAD SAUCE

WHAT'S BETTER THAN BREAD SAUCE? CHICKEN & BACON BAKED IN BREAD SAUCE, THAT'S WHAT. DO IT. TRUST ME

SERVES 4
PREP 10 MINUTES
COOK 50 MINUTES

1 onion

2½ cups whole milk

2 teaspoons English mustard

4 small bay leaves

2 large eggs

½ a nutmeg

2 cloves

10½ slices of bread
(10½ oz total)

4 large chicken thighs,
skin on, bone in

2 slices of smoked bacon

1 Preheat the oven to 350°F. Peel, halve and finely slice the onion, place in a 9 x 13-inch roasting pan with the milk, mustard, bay leaves and eggs, finely grate in the nutmeg and cloves, and add a pinch of sea salt and black pepper.

2 Slice the crusts off the bread and reserve, tear the middle of the bread into the roasting pan, then really scrunch and mix it all together. Dunk the reserved crusts in the mixture and arrange around the edge of the pan.

3 Rub the chicken thighs with a little salt, pepper and olive oil, then nestle them into the roasting pan, skin side up. Halve and add the bacon slices, and roast for 50 minutes, or until golden. Serve with seasonal greens.

VEGGIE LOVE ────────────────

Break 1 small cauliflower into chunky florets, leaving any nice leaves intact, toss in a little olive oil, salt and pepper, and use in place of the chicken and bacon. Grate in 3 oz of Cheddar cheese, then cover the pan with aluminum foil and roast as above, removing the foil halfway through cooking.

ENERGY	FAT	SAT FAT	PROTEIN	CARBS	SUGARS	SALT	FIBER
691kcal	32.7g	10.9g	40.6g	59.1g	14.6g	2.5g	4.1g

PANTRY LOVE

Sometimes, we all need a get-out-of-jail meal. Let the pantry shelves come to the rescue, offering mealtime inspiration when you need it most. You'll find some faithful friends here for your hour of need – ones you'll return to again and again.

BIGGING UP
BEANS

Readers, I have a confession – I love canned beans. They're a brilliant and tasty source of plant-based protein, they're budget-friendly, they live happily in the pantry for ages, they're easily accessible and they're full of fiber. Plus, they have a wonderful ability to take on flavors from all over the world, and growing beans is actually good for the planet. In the pages that follow you'll find my love letter to beans, and hopefully it will inspire you to have your own romance – you can, of course, mix up the beans you choose. I've used my favorite combos here, and I hope you'll discover yours. Whether you eat them straight from the bowl, serve them on toast or pair them with something else, like a piece of steamed fish, sausages, a chicken breast or a fried egg, you'll find the possibilities for deliciousness are endless.

PS: Jarred beans are also amazing. They're normally at least twice the price but I'd say they're twice as delicious, too.

CREAMY PINTO BEANS

SERVES 2 | 9 MINUTES

Peel **2 cloves of garlic**, trim **1 bunch of scallions**, finely slice it all and place in a non-stick frying pan on a medium heat with 1 tablespoon of olive oil. Fry for 2 minutes, pour in **1 x 15-oz can of pinto beans**, juice and all, followed by **6 tablespoons of crème fraîche**, and simmer until you have a silky sauce consistency. Season to perfection with sea salt and black pepper, finely grate and stir through **¾ oz of Parmesan or pecorino cheese**, then drizzle over a little extra virgin olive oil, if you like. Lovely served with roast chicken or piled into a steaming hot baked potato, or even with steamed or baked fish fillets.

ENERGY	FAT	SAT FAT	PROTEIN	CARBS	SUGARS	SALT	FIBER
435kcal	26g	13.9g	17g	34.6g	3.3g	0.2g	10.6g

GOCHUJANG BLACK BEANS

SERVES 2 | 10 MINUTES

Reserving the juice, drain **1 x 15-oz can of black beans** and tip them into a dry non-stick frying pan on a high heat to char and pop. Halve and add **5½ oz of ripe cherry tomatoes**, then trim and finely slice **1 bunch of scallions**, adding half to the frying pan, along with **1 tablespoon each of gochujang paste** and olive oil, the reserved bean juice and a few splashes of water. Cut **1 x 12-oz block of silken tofu** into big cubes, sit them in the beans, and simmer until you have a silky sauce consistency. Season to perfection with sea salt and black pepper, and scatter over the remaining scallion. Good with crusty bread.

ENERGY	FAT	SAT FAT	PROTEIN	CARBS	SUGARS	SALT	FIBER
302kcal	7.9g	1.8g	26g	25.5g	9.9g	1g	15g

191

ROSEMARY BORLOTTI BEANS

SERVES 2 | 14 MINUTES

Strip the leaves from **2 sprigs of rosemary**. Peel and very finely slice **2 cloves of garlic**. Use a vegetable peeler to strip the peel off **½ a lemon**. Place it all in a non-stick frying pan on a medium heat with 1 tablespoon of olive oil, shaking the frying pan regularly until crisp and lightly golden, then remove half. Add **2 anchovy fillets** to the frying pan, pour in **1 x 15-oz can of borlotti or pinto beans**, juice and all, and simmer until you have a silky sauce consistency. Season to perfection with sea salt and black pepper, then scatter over the crispy bits and serve. Try them with a soft-boiled egg and steamed spinach, or with mozzarella and tomatoes.

ENERGY	FAT	SAT FAT	PROTEIN	CARBS	SUGARS	SALT	FIBER
165kcal	7.4g	1.1g	9.8g	14.8g	0.7g	0.4g	7.6g

HARISSA BUTTER BEANS

SERVES 2 | 12 MINUTES

Peel **2 cloves of garlic** and finely slice with the stalks from **4 sprigs of Italian parsley**, reserving the leaves. Place the garlic and parsley stalks in a non-stick frying pan on a medium heat with 1 tablespoon of olive oil, stirring regularly until lightly golden. Pour in **1 x 15-oz can of butter beans**, juice and all, add **1 tablespoon of harissa paste**, and simmer until you have a silky sauce consistency. Add the juice of **½ a lemon**, season to perfection with sea salt and black pepper, finely chop and sprinkle with the parsley leaves, and serve with **lemon wedges**, for squeezing over. Nice with halloumi or mackerel.

ENERGY	FAT	SAT FAT	PROTEIN	CARBS	SUGARS	SALT	FIBER
191kcal	8.6g	1.3g	9.1g	19.3g	1.6g	0.1g	6.8g

PESTO CANNELLINI BEANS

SERVES 2–4 | 13 MINUTES

Trim **7 oz of fine green beans**, finely slice and place in a non-stick pan on a medium-high heat to lightly char one side only. Finely grate in the zest of **½ a lemon**, pour in **1 x 15-oz can of cannellini beans** (also known as white kidney beans), juice and all, bring to a boil, then squeeze in the **lemon juice** and season to perfection with sea salt and black pepper. When you have a silky sauce consistency, stir in **1 heaping tablespoon of pesto**, finely grate over **½ oz of Parmesan cheese** and serve. Great teamed with salmon or roasted eggplant.

ENERGY	FAT	SAT FAT	PROTEIN	CARBS	SUGARS	SALT	FIBER
201kcal	7.3g	1.9g	12.8g	17g	3.2g	0.8g	12.2g

SPICED NAVY BEANS

SERVES 2 | 16 MINUTES

Put a non-stick frying pan on a medium heat with 1 tablespoon of olive oil, finely chop the stalks from **4 sprigs of cilantro** (reserving the leaves) and add with **1 heaping tablespoon of korma curry paste** and **1 level teaspoon of ground turmeric**. Fry for 1 minute, pour in **1 x 15-oz can of navy beans**, juice and all, add **5½ oz of frozen leaf spinach**, bring to a boil, then simmer for 5 minutes, or until the spinach has thawed, stirring regularly and adding a splash of water, if needed. Season to perfection with red wine vinegar, sea salt and black pepper. Add the cilantro leaves. Nice with paneer.

ENERGY	FAT	SAT FAT	PROTEIN	CARBS	SUGARS	SALT	FIBER
215kcal	9.8g	2.3g	11g	22.4g	2.6g	0.5g	8.1g

BUSTED SAUSAGE ON TOAST WITH BEANS

BREAKFAST, BRUNCH, LUNCH OR DINNER, THIS 13-MINUTE TOAST & BEAN COMBO IS A GUARANTEED WINNER

SERVES 2

13 MINUTES

7 oz mixed mushrooms

2 large sausages (2½ oz each)

2 thick slices of bread

4 sprigs of thyme

2 tablespoons HP sauce

2 teaspoons sun-dried tomato paste

1 x 15-oz can of cannellini beans (also known as white kidney beans)

1 Place a large non-stick frying pan on a medium-high heat. Slice or tear the mushrooms into the frying pan to start dry-frying as it heats.

2 Squeeze the sausagemeat out of its casing, pressing and smoothing it to cover the whole surface of one side of each piece of bread, then place sausage-side down in the frying pan with a splash of olive oil and cook for 3 to 4 minutes on each side, or until golden and crisp, picking in the thyme halfway.

3 Generously brush the sausage side of each toast with HP sauce, flip to glaze for just 30 seconds, and remove to a plate with the mushrooms.

4 Add the sun-dried tomato paste and beans, juice and all, to the frying pan and simmer vigorously until reduced to a nice consistency. Season to perfection and serve alongside the toast and mushrooms.

VEGGIE LOVE —————————————————————

Simply swap in veggie sausages, mashing them onto the bread, and you're good to go.

ENERGY	FAT	SAT FAT	PROTEIN	CARBS	SUGARS	SALT	FIBER
509kcal	22.5g	7.4g	27.2g	44.1g	4.4g	1.6g	10.2g

SMOKY BACON BALSAMIC LIVER & BEANS

AN AMAZING SWEET & SOUR TAKE ON THE BRITISH CLASSIC, SERVED ON DELICIOUS CREAMY BEANS, IN NO TIME

SERVES 2
16 MINUTES

1 onion

2 slices of smoked bacon

2 sprigs of sage

1 x 15-oz can of butter beans

2 x 4½-oz slices of calves' or lamb's liver, each ½-inch thick (ask your butcher)

2 tablespoons balsamic vinegar

1 teaspoon liquid honey

1 Peel and very finely slice the onion, place in a large non-stick frying pan on a medium heat with 1 tablespoon of olive oil and a splash of water, and fry for 10 minutes, or until softened, stirring regularly.

2 Meanwhile, slice the bacon and place in another frying pan on a medium-high heat with a little drizzle of oil. Once lightly golden, pick in the sage and fry both until crispy, then remove with a slotted spoon, pouring the beans, juice and all, into the frying pan of tasty fat. Simmer for a few minutes until creamy, mashing a few beans, then season to perfection with sea salt and black pepper.

3 Push the onions to one side of the frying pan and turn the heat up to high. Slice the liver into ¾-inch strips, add to the frying pan and fry for 2 minutes, then go in with the balsamic and honey, toss well and season to perfection.

4 Divide the creamy beans between your plates, spoon over the liver and sticky onions, then finish with the crispy bacon and sage, and a drizzle of extra virgin olive oil, if you like.

ENERGY	FAT	SAT FAT	PROTEIN	CARBS	SUGARS	SALT	FIBER
420kcal	17.1g	3.8g	34g	32.8g	13.9g	0.5g	8.1g

JAZZING UP
JARRED
JALAPEÑOS

Here lies a little secret that I do quite regularly at home. It's an unbelievably simple way to turn an everyday pantry ingredient into something even more useful and with even more flavor. I've given you some inspiration for how to use it, so have a go, try it on some of your favorite things, create new ones, and enjoy!

EASY GREEN CHILI SALSA

Simply tip **1 x 12-oz jar of jalapeños**, liquid and all, into a blender, pick in **1 bunch of mint leaves (1½ oz)**, add **1½ tablespoons of liquid honey** and blitz until really smooth. Use as you will, pouring the rest back into the jar, where it will keep happily in the fridge for up to a week, ready to salsa up your meals.

CHEESE ON TOAST

SERVES 1 | 6 MINUTES

Place **1 slice of bread** under the broiler until golden on one side. Spread **1 tablespoon of Easy green chili salsa** (page 200) on the untoasted side of the bread, then grate over **1 oz of a nice melty cheese of your choice**. Pop back under the broiler until golden, oozy and melty. Cut into soldiers and serve with extra Easy green chili salsa.

ENERGY	FAT	SAT FAT	PROTEIN	CARBS	SUGARS	SALT	FIBER
218kcal	10.9g	6.6g	11.2g	18.3g	1.8g	1.3g	0g

SCRAMBLED EGGS

SERVES 2 | 5 MINUTES

Beat **5 eggs** with a pinch of sea salt and black pepper. Place **1 knob of unsalted butter** in a small non-stick frying pan on a medium heat, then, once melted, pour in the eggs. Stir slowly with a spatula, moving them around so you get waves of silky egg curds, then remove from the heat before the eggs are fully cooked, as they will continue to cook in the residual heat of the frying pan. Serve on **hot buttered toast**, with a nice dollop of **Easy green chili salsa** (page 200) on the side.

ENERGY	FAT	SAT FAT	PROTEIN	CARBS	SUGARS	SALT	FIBER
307kcal	18.1g	6g	19.1g	17.9g	1.3g	1.5g	0g

BAKED FETA

SERVES 4 AS A SIDE | 20 MINUTES

Preheat the oven to 350°F. Place **1 x 7-oz block of feta** in a baking dish, season with black pepper, then bake for 20 minutes, or until golden. With 10 minutes to go, place a large non-stick frying pan on a high heat. Drizzle in a little olive oil, sprinkle in **2 cups of frozen corn**, then trim, finely slice and add **2 scallions**. Once the corn is nicely charred on one side, turn the heat off. Spoon ¼ **cup of Easy green chili salsa** (page 200) onto a plate, break over the baked feta, then sprinkle with the corn and scallions. Nice with wraps.

ENERGY	FAT	SAT FAT	PROTEIN	CARBS	SUGARS	SALT	FIBER
229kcal	14.4g	7.5g	10.6g	17.2g	4.5g	1.7g	2.1g

PUNCHY SHRIMP

SERVES 2 | 9 MINUTES

Peel and slice **2 cloves of garlic**. Peel **8 raw shell-on jumbo shrimp**, leaving the heads and tails intact, then run a small sharp knife down the back of each to butterfly it, also removing the vein. Place the shrimp in a non-stick frying pan on a medium-high heat with 2 tablespoons of olive oil and cook for 3 to 4 minutes, or until the shrimp are just cooked, shaking the frying pan constantly and adding the garlic and the leaves from **a few sprigs of oregano** for the final minute. Squeeze over the juice of **½ a lemon** and serve on top of **3 tablespoons of Easy green chili salsa** (page 200).

ENERGY	FAT	SAT FAT	PROTEIN	CARBS	SUGARS	SALT	FIBER
173kcal	13.6g	2g	10.5g	2.5g	1.7g	0.9g	0.4g

QUICK CEVICHE

SERVES 4 AS A STARTER | 5 MINUTES, PLUS CHILLING

Dice **9 oz of super-fresh skinless boneless white fish fillets** into ½-inch cubes and finely chop **½ a small red onion**, then toss with a generous pinch of sea salt and the **juice from 2 limes**. Refrigerate for 30 minutes, then separate out **1 little gem lettuce** to create edible cups and arrange on plates. Spoon over the cured fish, drizzle each portion with **Easy green chili salsa** (page 200) and extra virgin olive oil, to taste, then scatter over **a few baby mint leaves**, to finish.

ENERGY	FAT	SAT FAT	PROTEIN	CARBS	SUGARS	SALT	FIBER
156kcal	4.6g	0.7g	24.3g	4.5g	3.9g	1.1g	1.7g

CHICKEN LOLLIPOPS

A FUN & EASY WAY TO QUICKLY COOK CHICKEN THIGHS, WITH A CLEVER DOUBLE USE OF EASY GREEN CHILI SALSA

SERVES 2
20 MINUTES
PLUS MARINATING

4 skinless boneless
    chicken thighs

¼ cup Easy green chili salsa
    (page 200)

½ a red onion

2 flatbreads

1 sprig of mint

1 Halve the chicken thighs, toss with 2 tablespoons of salsa and a little olive oil and marinate in the fridge for 2 hours, or even overnight. Soak four wooden skewers in water for an hour or so before using, to prevent them from burning.

2 When you're ready to cook, peel and very finely slice the onion, scrunch with a good pinch of sea salt and 2 tablespoons of red wine vinegar, then set aside to quickly pickle.

3 Divide, fold and skewer two pieces of chicken onto each of the four wooden skewers (you may need to trim your skewers to fit your grill pan). Cook in a hot grill pan, or under a hot broiler, for 12 to 14 minutes, or until cooked through, turning regularly.

4 Warm the flatbreads. Spread 1 tablespoon of salsa across each one, then add a pair of skewers. Sprinkle with the red onion pickle, tear over a few baby mint leaves, then remove the skewers, roll and wrap. Great with a little salad.

AIR-FRYER IT —————————————————————

Cook the chicken skewers in a single layer in an air fryer at 400°F, trimming your skewers and cooking in batches if needed, for 20 minutes, or until cooked through, turning halfway.

ENERGY	FAT	SAT FAT	PROTEIN	CARBS	SUGARS	SALT	FIBER
474kcal	16.9g	3.6g	36.8g	42.4g	6.1g	1.7g	2.6g

CELEBRATING CHICKPEAS

From frumpy to fashionable, chickpeas are having a moment and there's a good reason for it. Not only are they a great high-fiber, plant-based protein, they're a fantastic legume that you can fry, roast or stew, smash into paste or turn into sauces, flavoring as you will with spices from all over the world. Whether you choose canned, jarred or even dried, all of us embracing this legume in our lives is only going to be good for us, and for the planet. So, please enjoy a handful of my favorite chickpea recipes that we eat all the time at home.

CHICKPEA CHOPPED SALAD

CANNED CHICKPEAS ARE DOUBLY TRANSFORMED INTO SILKEN HUMMUS & CRISPY BITES FOR BONUS TEXTURE

SERVES 4

15 MINUTES

2 x 15-oz cans of chickpeas

1 teaspoon dukkah

1 clove of garlic

1 lemon

¼ cup tahini

1¼ lbs crunchy veg, such
    as English cucumber, bell
    pepper, fennel, radishes,
    tomatoes

1 bunch of tarragon (¾ oz)

1 Pour 1 can of chickpeas, juice and all, into a blender, then drain the second can and add half to the blender. Put the rest into a non-stick frying pan on a medium-high heat with 1 tablespoon of olive oil, tossing regularly, and, once crispy, sprinkle in the dukkah and toss until fragrant.

2 Peel the garlic and add to the blender, squeeze in the lemon juice, add the tahini and blitz until smooth, then season to perfection with sea salt and black pepper. Divide and spread across four serving plates.

3 Prep your chosen veg, pick the tarragon, then chop it all together on a large board until fairly fine, mixing as you go. Drizzle with 2 tablespoons each of red wine vinegar and extra virgin olive oil, mix well, season to perfection and pile on top of the hummus.

4 Scatter the hot crispy chickpeas over the salads and add a drizzle of extra virgin olive oil, if you like. Great with hot toast, for scooping and dunking.

ENERGY	FAT	SAT FAT	PROTEIN	CARBS	SUGARS	SALT	FIBER
344kcal	22.1g	3.2g	12.5g	23.8g	5.1g	0.5g	8.4g

FRAGRANT SPICED CHICKPEAS

SERVES 4 | 24 MINUTES

Put a large shallow Dutch oven on a medium-high heat with **¼ cup of Kerala curry paste or your favorite mild curry paste** and 1 tablespoon of olive oil. Chop and add **1 lb of ripe tomatoes**. Cook and stir for 5 minutes, then drain and add **1 x 24-oz jar of chickpeas** and pour in **1 x 13½-oz can of reduced-fat coconut milk**. Simmer for 15 minutes, or until thickened to a nice consistency, mashing some of the chickpeas and stirring occasionally. Stir in **1 tablespoon of mango chutney** and season to perfection with sea salt and black pepper.

ENERGY	FAT	SAT FAT	PROTEIN	CARBS	SUGARS	SALT	FIBER
317kcal	15.9g	6.3g	11.4g	32.5g	9.3g	0.7g	9.3g

GENNARO'S CHICKPEAS

SERVES 2-4 | 15 MINUTES

Peel and finely slice **2 cloves of garlic**, then place in a large shallow Dutch oven on a medium-high heat with 1 tablespoon of olive oil. Strip in the leaves from **2 sprigs of rosemary** and fry until crispy. Stir in **2 tablespoons of sun-dried tomato paste**, then pour in **1 x 24-oz jar of chickpeas**, juice and all, and ¾ cup of water. Bring to a boil, simmer for 5 minutes, then tear in **8 oz of kale**, discarding any thicker stalks. Cover and cook for 5 minutes, or until the kale has wilted, adding an extra splash of water, if needed. Season to perfection with sea salt and black pepper.

ENERGY	FAT	SAT FAT	PROTEIN	CARBS	SUGARS	SALT	FIBER
444kcal	17.3g	2.6g	23.6g	48.6g	3.5g	0.5g	14.4g

SQUASH & CHICKPEA SOUP

SOMETIMES ALL WE NEED IS A COMFORTING SEASONAL SOUP TO PICK US UP & GIVE US A DELICIOUS FOOD HUG

SERVES 6
55 MINUTES

1 butternut squash (2½ lbs)

2 onions

2 stalks of celery

½ oz dried porcini mushrooms

2 x 15-oz cans of chickpeas

2 veg or chicken bouillon cubes

9 oz random dried pasta

2 sprigs of rosemary

1½ oz Parmesan cheese

1 Carefully halve the squash lengthwise, seed, then chop into ½-inch dice and place in a large shallow Dutch oven on a medium heat with 2 tablespoons of olive oil, stirring occasionally.

2 Peel the onions, trim the celery, chop into ½-inch dice and add to the Dutch oven, then finely chop and add the dried mushrooms. Cook for 15 minutes, or until starting to color, continuing to stir occasionally.

3 Pour in the chickpeas, juice and all. Make and add 5 cups of hot broth and simmer for 15 minutes, then remove a quarter of the soup to a blender, blitz until smooth and stir back into the Dutch oven along with the pasta.

4 Cook for another 15 minutes, or until the pasta is cooked and the soup has thickened nicely, adding a splash of water, if needed, then season to perfection with sea salt, black pepper and a little swig of red wine vinegar.

5 Strip the rosemary leaves into a mortar and pestle, pound into a paste with a small pinch of salt, then muddle in ¼ cup of extra virgin olive oil. Serve the soup drizzled with the oil, and with a grating of Parmesan.

ENERGY	FAT	SAT FAT	PROTEIN	CARBS	SUGARS	SALT	FIBER
456kcal	17.6g	3.4g	16g	62.9g	12.6g	1.2g	8.1g

SAVING
TORTILLAS

Tortillas are available everywhere and I'm often asked for fun ways
to use them up – they seem to be one of those ingredients that some
people buy and leave languishing at the bottom of the bread box. So as
one of the most popular but also potentially the most wasted food items,
I hope the recipes that follow will get you excited about using them.
Let's get creative and have some fun with tortillas.

QUESADILLA TOASTED SANDWICH

I LOVE A TOASTED SANDWICH, BUT THIS ONE MIXES IT UP IN A WONDERFUL WAY – IT'S A NEW FAVORITE FOR ME

SERVES 2

15 MINUTES

4 regular flour tortillas

2 eggs

2 teaspoons chili & garlic or
   your favorite curry paste

½ an English cucumber

1 lime

2 scallions

¼ cup plain yogurt

2 tablespoons unsweetened
   shredded coconut

1 Preheat your panini press. Carefully push two tortillas into the base of the machine, making a nice dip in the middle of each one, then gently crack in the eggs.

2 Spread the remaining two tortillas with the curry paste, then flip on top of the eggs, carefully fold in any overhang, seal the machine, and toast for 10 minutes, or until golden.

3 Very finely slice the cucumber, toss with half the lime juice and a good pinch of sea salt, and leave to quickly pickle. Trim and finely slice the scallions, mix most of them into the yogurt with the coconut and remaining lime juice, then season to perfection with salt and black pepper.

4 Trim and slice up the quesadilla toasted sandwich, spoon over the flavored yogurt and quick-pickled cucumber, then sprinkle with the rest of the scallions.

ENERGY	FAT	SAT FAT	PROTEIN	CARBS	SUGARS	SALT	FIBER
347kcal	14.2g	5.6g	15.6g	39.6g	7.1g	1.4g	1.4g

CAJUN-SPICED ENCHILADAS

THINK YOU'VE GOT NOTHING FOR DINNER? HUMBLE CANS & FREEZER FRIENDS HELP TO DELIVER BIG IN THIS TASTY DISH

SERVES 4–6
PREP 20 MINUTES
COOK 30 MINUTES

2 large sweet potatoes
(12 oz each)

2 cloves of garlic

4 teaspoons Cajun seasoning

2 x 14-oz cans of plum
tomatoes

2¾ cups frozen corn

1 bunch of scallions

8 soft corn tortillas

1 x 15-oz can of black beans

1¼ cups cottage cheese

optional: chili sauce, to serve

1 Preheat the oven to 350°F. Scrub the sweet potatoes, prick all over with a fork, then microwave on full power for 12 minutes, or until soft.

2 Peel and finely slice the garlic, then fry in a large non-stick frying pan on a medium-high heat with 1 tablespoon of olive oil until lightly golden, stirring regularly. Stir in 1 teaspoon of Cajun seasoning, followed 1 minute later by the tomatoes, breaking them up with your spoon. Simmer for 5 minutes, then season to perfection with sea salt and black pepper.

3 Pour the tomato sauce into a 9 x 13-inch roasting pan, wipe out the frying pan, then dry-fry the corn on a high heat until charred. Trim and finely slice the scallions, adding just the whites to the roasting pan with 1 teaspoon of Cajun seasoning, and removing from the heat once lightly golden.

4 Quarter the sweet potatoes lengthwise and smash one quarter into each tortilla, spoon over the corn mix, then roll up and nestle into the sauce.

5 Drain the beans, toss with the remaining 2 teaspoons of Cajun seasoning and 1 tablespoon of red wine vinegar, then scatter over the tortillas, spoon over the cottage cheese, drizzle with 1 tablespoon of oil and bake for 30 minutes, or until golden and bubbling.

6 Finish with the reserved green scallions, and chili sauce, if you like.

ENERGY	FAT	SAT FAT	PROTEIN	CARBS	SUGARS	SALT	FIBER
651kcal	16.8g	4.7g	26g	97.3g	28.2g	1.6g	16g

GOLDEN LAMB TORTILLA & CRUNCH SALAD

FROM ZERO TO HERO IN JUST 10 MINUTES, THIS FLAVOR-PACKED LUNCH FOR ONE IS A SURPRISING DELIGHT

SERVES 1

10 MINUTES

¼ of a red onion

1 teaspoon fennel seeds

4½ oz ground lamb

1 large whole wheat tortilla

2 sprigs of mint

½ a fresh red chili

5½ oz crunchy veg, such as
English cucumber, bell
pepper, red onion, radish,
carrot

1 teaspoon liquid honey

1 teaspoon shelled unsalted
pistachios

1 Peel the onion and finely chop with the fennel seeds, scrunch and mix well with the lamb, season with sea salt and black pepper, then squash and spread the mixture across the tortilla.

2 Place the tortilla lamb-side down in a large frying pan on a medium-high heat and cook for 5 minutes, or until the lamb is golden and the tortilla is dark and crisp at the edges, twisting it occasionally in the lovely fat in the frying pan.

3 Pick the mint leaves into a bowl. Finely slice and add the chili. Prep and finely slice or peel the crunchy veg so they're delicate and a pleasure to eat, then add to the bowl and dress with a little red wine vinegar and extra virgin olive oil, and season to perfection.

4 Flip the golden tortilla out of the frying pan, drizzle with the honey, pile the salad on top, then chop and scatter over the pistachios, and enjoy.

ENERGY	FAT	SAT FAT	PROTEIN	CARBS	SUGARS	SALT	FIBER
515kcal	25.8g	8g	33.2g	38.9g	12.3g	1.2g	7.4g

CHEESY BLACK BEAN NACHOS

IF YOU'VE GOT A GAS STOVE, THE CHARRING STAGE ADDS SO MUCH FLAVOR TO THESE SPEEDY HAND-TORN NACHOS

SERVES 4

19 MINUTES

4 large whole wheat tortillas

1 x 15-oz can of black beans

2 teaspoons Cajun seasoning

2 oz Cheddar cheese

5½ oz ripe tomatoes

1–2 tablespoons chipotle
   hot sauce

1 bunch of chives (¾ oz)

¼ cup sour cream

1 lemon

1 Preheat the broiler to high. Toast the tortillas over the flame of a gas burner (or toast in a hot, dry frying pan), turning with tongs until starting to catch, then tear into a large roasting pan.

2 Drain the beans, toss with the Cajun seasoning and 1 tablespoon of olive oil, then scatter over the tortillas, using a fork to squash them down. Grate over the cheese and broil for 3 to 5 minutes, or until golden and crisp.

3 In a blender, blitz the tomatoes with 1 tablespoon each of extra virgin olive oil and red wine vinegar, then add the hot sauce, sea salt and black pepper to taste. Decant into a bowl, adding extra chili sauce, if you like.

4 Rinse out the blender, then blitz the chives with the sour cream and lemon juice, saving a few chives for garnish, if you like. Season to perfection and pour into a second bowl. Serve with the nachos, and get dunking!

ENERGY	FAT	SAT FAT	PROTEIN	CARBS	SUGARS	SALT	FIBER
381kcal	18.1g	7.6g	14.5g	35.1g	4.9g	1.6g	10.9g

TASTY TORTILLA TAGLIATELLE

IF YOU'VE RUN OUT OF PASTA BUT STILL WANT THAT COMFORTING VIBE, THIS IS FOR YOU. TRUST ME, IT'S A THING

SERVES 2
15 MINUTES

2 large flour tortillas

2 cloves of garlic

½–1 fresh red chili

1 x 14-oz can of plum
   tomatoes

8 black olives (with pits)

½ x 4½-oz ball of mozzarella

2 sprigs of basil

1 Warm the tortillas in a large non-stick frying pan on a high heat for just 20 seconds, so you can roll them up tight and slice into ½-inch-thick strips. Sprinkle back into the frying pan, tossing until crisp and golden, then remove.

2 Peel the garlic and finely slice with the chili. Turn down the heat to medium, then go in with 1 tablespoon of olive oil, the garlic and chili and fry until lightly golden, stirring regularly.

3 Tip in the tomatoes, breaking them up with your spoon, quarter-fill the can with water, swirl around and pour into the frying pan, then simmer for 5 minutes and season to perfection with sea salt and black pepper.

4 Toss the crispy tortillas through the sauce, tear over the olives, discarding the pits, mozzarella and basil leaves, and drizzle with a little extra virgin olive oil, if you like. Serve with a green salad.

ENERGY	FAT	SAT FAT	PROTEIN	CARBS	SUGARS	SALT	FIBER
352kcal	16.4g	6.6g	13.6g	36.1g	10.1g	1.6g	5.8g

QUESADILLA SALAD BOWL

THERE'S SOMETHING SUPER-SATISFYING ABOUT SHARING CRUNCHY FRESH SALAD IN A CHEESY QUESADILLA

SERVES 2
10 MINUTES

2½ oz Cheddar cheese

2 large flour tortillas

1 scallion

½ cup canned corn

7 oz salad veg, such as English
   cucumber, carrot, bell
   pepper, chili, endive,
   arugula, spinach, radishes,
   red onion

2 sprigs of mint

1 Place a large non-stick frying pan on a medium-high heat. Grate half the cheese over one of the tortillas. Finely chop and sprinkle over the scallion, scatter over the corn, grate over the remaining cheese, then press the remaining tortilla on top.

2 Cook for 2 minutes on each side, or until golden, then while still warm, push the quesadilla into a shallow bowl to create yourself an edible bowl.

3 As it cooks, prepare your salad veg so they're delicate and a pleasure to eat – I use vegetable peelers and crinkle cutters to have a bit of fun. Pick and finely chop the mint, add to the salad, and dress with 1 tablespoon each of red wine vinegar and extra virgin olive oil, and a pinch of sea salt and black pepper.

4 Pile the salad inside your quesadilla bowl, and serve.

ENERGY	FAT	SAT FAT	PROTEIN	CARBS	SUGARS	SALT	FIBER
430kcal	23.8g	10.5g	16.9g	36.5g	5g	1.8g	3.7g

HOT & CRISPY ICE CREAM PARCEL

TORTILLAS WORK WITH SWEET THINGS, TOO, & THIS IS ONE OF THE QUICKEST DESSERTS YOU CAN MAKE – JOYFUL!

SERVES 1
4 MINUTES

1 regular flour tortilla

1 ripe banana

1 heaping tablespoon Nutella

1 small scoop (¼ cup) vanilla
    ice cream

1 knob of unsalted butter

1 tablespoon maple syrup

ground cinnamon, for dusting

1 Warm the tortilla in a non-stick frying pan on a medium heat for just 20 seconds, then remove. Peel the banana, halve it lengthwise and place cut side down in the frying pan.

2 Spread the Nutella in the center of the tortilla, sit the scoop of ice cream on top, then fold in the sides of the tortilla to cover the filling.

3 Add the butter to the frying pan, let it melt, then add the tortilla parcel, folded side down, for just 1 minute, or until golden. Flip with the banana for another minute, then plate up.

4 Tease open the tortilla, drizzle with the maple syrup, and serve right away with a sprinkling of cinnamon, to taste.

ENERGY	FAT	SAT FAT	PROTEIN	CARBS	SUGARS	SALT	FIBER
607kcal	26.1g	14g	9.7g	82.5g	49.8g	0.7g	4.9g

DELICIOUS DESSERTS

Because we all deserve a sweet treat every now and then. And, of course, these recipes are still full of my tips, tricks and shortcuts, so it's easy to make something delicious to share with your loved ones, if you want to share, that is . . .

BANOFFEE FRO-YO TART

YOU'VE GOT TO TRY THIS REIMAGINING OF THE BRITISH CLASSIC. IT'S FAST, IT'S FUN & WILL MAKE YOU GO OOOOH . . .

SERVES 10
15 MINUTES
PLUS CHILLING & FREEZING

7 oz soft pitted dates

2 cups sliced almonds

½ teaspoon ground cinnamon

½ x 13½-oz can of
  dulce de leche

2 ripe bananas (7 oz total)

½ a lime

2 teaspoons vanilla bean paste

2 cups Greek yogurt

1¾ oz dark chocolate (70%)

1 For the base, blitz the dates, almonds and cinnamon in a food processor until fine and tacky, then tip onto a large sheet of parchment paper, fold the paper over, and use a rolling pin to roll out to a rectangle about 10 x 14 inches and just under ¼-inch thick.

2 Gently lift – paper and all – into a 9 x 13-inch baking pan, easing it into the corners and using the back of a spoon to push it up the sides. Evenly spread the dulce de leche across the base. Peel and slice the bananas, toss with the finely grated zest and juice of the lime, then layer them over the dulce de leche. Mix the vanilla into the yogurt and spoon over the top.

3 Place the tart in the fridge, until an hour before you want to serve, then transfer it to the freezer for 1 hour so it becomes softly set but still sliceable. Serve straightaway, with shavings or gratings of chocolate.

ENERGY	FAT	SAT FAT	PROTEIN	CARBS	SUGARS	SALT	FIBER
328kcal	17.3g	5.5g	9.1g	37.8g	31.8g	0.1g	4.5g

5-MINUTE FRO-YO

GOT THE URGE FOR SOMETHING SWEET & SATISFYING? THIS FAST, NUTRITIOUS BEAUTY WILL HIT THE SPOT

SERVES 6–8
5 MINUTES
PLUS FREEZING

2 ripe bananas (7 oz total)

1 lb frozen fruit

2 cups plain yogurt or
    crème fraîche

2 tablespoons elderflower
    cordial

1 Peel, slice and freeze the bananas, ideally in advance.

2 In a food processor, pulse the bananas with your chosen frozen fruit, the plain yogurt or crème fraîche and elderflower cordial until smooth, stopping halfway to scrape down the sides with a spatula and help it along.

3 Portion up what you want to eat now into bowls or cones, then freeze the rest in a suitable container.

4 If leaving it overnight or longer, once you're ready to serve, move it from the freezer to the fridge to gently thaw before tucking in.

ENERGY	FAT	SAT FAT	PROTEIN	CARBS	SUGARS	SALT	FIBER
302kcal	15.5g	5.3g	3.9g	44.5g	22.3g	0.4g	1.6g

EASIEST ICE CREAM

A NO-CHURN METHOD THAT MEANS MINIMUM EFFORT & YOU CAN FLAVOR IT HOWEVER YOUR HEART DESIRES

SERVES 12
PREP 9 MINUTES
FREEZE 4 HOURS
THAW 30 MINUTES

2½ cups heavy cream

1 x 14-oz can of
condensed milk

FLAVOR OPTIONS – CHOOSE ONE

1 cup Maltesers or Whoppers

3 x mint Aeros or other
mint chocolate bars

½ a jar of apricot jam

½ a jar of raspberry jam
& 7 oz raspberries

1 In a large bowl, whisk the cream until soft peaks form, then fold in the condensed milk until evenly combined.

2 Choose your flavor option. If using Maltesers, Whoppers or Aeros, bash them up into different sizes – small bits, big bits and dusty bits, for variety – and fold most of them into the ice cream mixture, reserving a small handful. If using jam or fruit, swirl and ripple it through, reserving a few berries to decorate.

3 Line a freezer-safe container or loaf pan with a sheet of scrunched-up damp parchment paper and pour in the mixture, making sure it gets into all the corners, then sprinkle over the reserved chocolate or berries, cover and freeze for at least 4 hours, or until set.

4 To serve, move from freezer to fridge 30 minutes to 1 hour before you want to eat it, and gently thaw to a sliceable consistency. Turn out onto a board, remove the parchment paper and carefully slice with a warm knife.

EASY SWAPS

Experiment with your favorite chocolate bars here, and swap in any jams, curds or fresh fruit you want to try. This recipe is fantastic for experimenting and having lots of fun.

ENERGY	FAT	SAT FAT	PROTEIN	CARBS	SUGARS	SALT	FIBER
379kcal	30g	18.7g	3.9g	24.4g	23.5g	0.2g	0.1g

FABULOUS CANNED FRUIT GRANITAS

CONVENIENT, AFFORDABLE & ACCESSIBLE, CANNED FRUIT & SOME CLEVER COMBOS MEAN TASTY DESSERTS, WITH EASE

EACH SERVES 6
PREP 5 MINUTES
FREEZE 5 HOURS

MANDARIN

1 x 11-oz can of mandarins in syrup

2 tablespoons Campari

CHERRY

1 x 15-oz can of black cherries in syrup

2 tablespoons Scotch whisky

STRAWBERRY

1 x 14-oz can of strawberries in syrup

3 tablespoons elderflower cordial

juice of ½ a lemon

PEAR

1 x 15¼-oz can of pears in syrup

¾-inch piece of ginger (peeled)

juice of ½ a lemon

PINEAPPLE

1 x 20-oz can of pineapple in syrup

juice of 1 lime

APRICOT

1 x 15-oz can of apricots in syrup

1 teaspoon vanilla bean paste

1 Choose your combo, place the ingredients in a food processor or blender and blitz until smooth – have a taste and tweak with a little **sugar**, if needed.

2 Tip into a shallow 8-inch freezer-safe dish (I like to use enamel or stoneware that will look nice on the table) and freeze for 5 hours, then cover and leave in the freezer until required.

3 To serve, use two forks to scrape the granita into ice crystals to order at the table – you'll need to work quickly but it's worth it! Delicious served with whipped cream, yogurt, crème fraîche or custard. It'll keep happily in the freezer for up to 3 months.

ENERGY	FAT	SAT FAT	PROTEIN	CARBS	SUGARS	SALT	FIBER
40kcal	0g	0g	0.2g	8g	7.7g	0g	0.3g

THESE VALUES ARE BASED ON THE MANDARIN COMBO ABOVE.

HERO
CHOCOLATE
CAKE

These next few pages are dedicated, with love, to my dear wife, Jools, who may just be one of the most chocolate-obsessed humans I have ever met in my life. What I'm giving you is a really indulgent, rich chocolate cake, which by good fortune happens to be gluten-free (which will also please Poppy and Petal). From this fine, delectable cake, you can go in a variety of different and surprising ways – and I have to say, the tiramisù is game-changing. Whichever recipe you choose to try first, the brilliant thing is that the cook time is always just 15 minutes, so even if you're short on time, there's always an enticing dessert waiting just around the corner.

DECADENT CHOCOLATE CAKE

FLOURLESS, RICH & OH-SO DELICIOUS, THIS CHOCOLATE-PACKED CAKE RECIPE IS ONE WE ALL NEED

SERVES 16
PREP 20 MINUTES
COOK 15 MINUTES

10½ oz dark chocolate (70%)

7 tablespoons unsalted butter

8 large eggs

1 cup superfine sugar

2 tablespoons unsweetened
   cocoa powder

1 Preheat the oven to 350°F. Snap the chocolate into a large heatproof bowl, add the butter and melt over a saucepan of gently simmering water, stirring regularly and making sure the water doesn't touch the base of the bowl, then leave to cool slightly.

2 Separate the eggs, putting the yolks into the bowl of a stand mixer with the superfine sugar, or into a large bowl if using a hand blender with a whisk attachment. Whisk for 2 minutes, or until pale and fluffy, then stir in the melted chocolate.

3 Whisk the egg whites and a pinch of sea salt in a separate bowl until stiff, using the stand mixer or hand blender. Working in batches, gently fold them into the chocolate mixture, then sift and fold in the cocoa.

4 Depending on your chosen recipe (pages 246 to 252), either pour the cake batter directly into a greased 9 x 13-inch baking pan or spread evenly across a 12 x 16-inch parchment-paper-lined rimmed baking sheet.

5 Bake for 15 minutes exactly – until just springy to the touch and gooey in the middle. Remove from the oven, and follow the rest of your recipe.

ENERGY	FAT	SAT FAT	PROTEIN	CARBS	SUGARS	SALT	FIBER
238kcal	13.9g	7.5g	4.9g	25.3g	24.9g	0.2g	0.8g

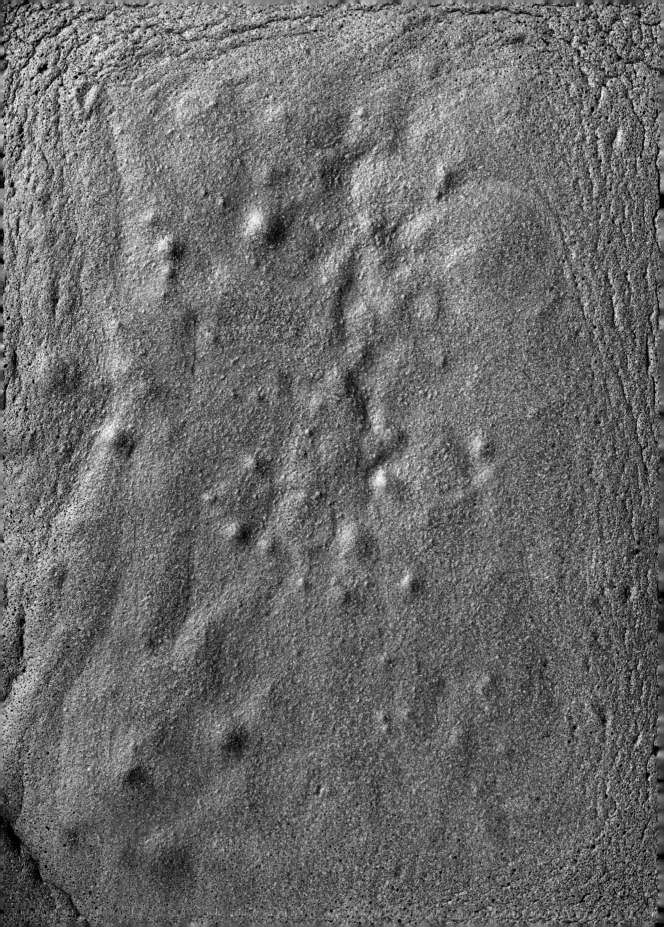

CHOCOLATE TIRAMISÙ

I'M A BIG TIRAMISÙ FAN & THIS EVOLVED TRIBUTE IS QUITE HONESTLY A DELIGHT – IT'S SIMPLY DELICIOUS

SERVES 16

42 MINUTES

PLUS COOLING

1 x Decadent chocolate cake
   (page 244)

⅔ cup strong coffee

3 tablespoons Cointreau

2 cups ricotta cheese

2½ cups mascarpone cheese

2 teaspoons vanilla bean paste

2 tablespoons superfine sugar

½ an orange

unsweetened cocoa powder,
   for dusting

1 Make the Decadent chocolate cake (page 244) and bake directly in a greased 9 x 13-inch baking pan at 350°F for 15 minutes exactly – until just springy to the touch and gooey in the middle.

2 Stab the sponge a few times with a skewer or sharp knife, evenly pour over the coffee and Cointreau, then leave to cool.

3 In a large bowl, mix the ricotta, mascarpone, vanilla paste and sugar, whisking until silky smooth, then spread over the soaked cake. Get creative with the side of a spatula or cake slice to make a fun pattern on the top.

4 Finely grate over the orange zest, top with a dusting of cocoa powder, and you're ready to serve. If you want to go extra indulgent, add a grating or scraping of dark chocolate instead of the cocoa.

GET AHEAD

This will sit happily in the fridge for up to 2 days at the end of step 3. Simply add the orange zest and cocoa powder to serve.

ENERGY	FAT	SAT FAT	PROTEIN	CARBS	SUGARS	SALT	FIBER
434kcal	31.3g	18.8g	9.3g	29.3g	28.9g	0.3g	0.7g

CAKE & DOUBLE CUSTARD

SERVES 12 | 38 MINUTES

Make the **Decadent chocolate cake** (page 244) and bake in a greased 9 x 13-inch baking pan at 350°F for 15 minutes exactly – until just springy to the touch and gooey in the middle. Serve hot from the oven as a dessert with double custard: serve up **1 x 14-oz can (1½ cups) of custard** cold from the can (or even better, chilled from the fridge), and heat another **1 x 14-oz can (1½ cups) of custard** with **1¾ oz of dark chocolate (70%)** to create a hot chocolate custard. Ripple away over the cake, and indulge.

ENERGY	FAT	SAT FAT	PROTEIN	CARBS	SUGARS	SALT	FIBER
403kcal	21.6g	11.7g	8.6g	46.4g	43.1g	0.3g	1.3g

ICE CREAM SANDWICHES

MAKES 18 | **25 MINUTES, PLUS FREEZING**

Make the **Decadent chocolate cake** (page 244) and bake on a 12 x 16-inch parchment-paper-lined rimmed baking sheet at 350°F for 15 minutes exactly – until just springy to the touch and gooey in the middle. Leave to cool, then cut the cake in half and freeze for 1 hour. Leave **1 x 1-pint container of vanilla ice cream** to soften just enough that you can spread it over one cake, then top with the second cake, press down and refreeze for 1 hour. Carefully slice into 18 pieces, and serve with a **jam of your choice**, for dunking.

ENERGY	FAT	SAT FAT	PROTEIN	CARBS	SUGARS	SALT	FIBER
260kcal	15g	8.7g	5.1g	27.8g	27.4g	0.2g	0.8g

BLACK FOREST ROLL

ALL THE BIG FLAVORS OF THE CLASSIC GÂTEAU BUT IN A MUCH EASIER TO MAKE, CUTE, CROWD-PLEASING ROLL

SERVES 16

48 MINUTES

PLUS COOLING

1 x Decadent chocolate cake
  (page 244)

unsweetened cocoa powder,
  for dusting

2½ cups heavy cream

2 teaspoons vanilla bean paste

1 tablespoon confectioner's
  sugar

1 x 13-oz jar of cherry
  preserves

½ x 13½-oz jar of black
  cherries in kirsch, bourbon
  or Scotch whisky

¾ cup roasted chopped
  hazelnuts

1 Make the Decadent chocolate cake (page 244) and bake on a 12 x 16-inch parchment-paper-lined rimmed baking sheet at 350°F for 15 minutes exactly – until just springy to the touch and gooey in the middle. Confidently turn out onto parchment paper dusted generously with cocoa. Leave to cool completely.

2 In a large bowl, whisk the cream and vanilla until soft peaks form, then sift and stir in the confectioner's sugar.

3 Peel away the parchment the cake was baked on. Spread the jam all over the cake, drizzle with kirsch juice from the cherry jar and spread over three-quarters of the cream. Scatter over most of the hazelnuts and cherries.

4 Tightly roll up the filled sponge lengthwise, using the base parchment to help you (it will bust and crack a bit, but it's all good).

5 Decorate the roll with the remaining cream and cherries, shave over extra chocolate, if you like, sprinkle over the remaining hazelnuts and drizzle with 2 tablespoons of kirsch juice. Serve right away, or pop in the fridge until needed. If making ahead, remove from the fridge 20 minutes before serving.

ENERGY	FAT	SAT FAT	PROTEIN	CARBS	SUGARS	SALT	FIBER
495kcal	34.4g	19.5g	6.1g	42.5g	37.5g	0.1g	1.3g

QUICK PARTY CAKE

THIS CAKE IS UNASSUMING BUT VERY DELICIOUS, & SUPER-EASY TO TRANSPORT FOR A HAPPY SURPRISE

SERVES 16+

27 MINUTES

PLUS COOLING

1 x Decadent chocolate cake (page 244)

½ cup plus 2 tablespoons soft unsalted butter

1¾ cups confectioner's sugar

¼ cup unsweetened cocoa powder

2 tablespoons milk

sprinkles of your choice

1 Make the Decadent chocolate cake (page 244) and bake directly in a greased 9 x 13-inch baking pan at 350°F for 15 minutes exactly — until just springy to the touch and gooey in the middle. Leave to cool. If you're going to want to lift it out of the pan to serve, line the pan with a scrunched-up sheet of damp parchment paper before you add the cake mix to make it easier to lift.

2 To make the buttercream, whisk the butter in a stand mixer, or in a large bowl with a hand blender with a whisk attachment, for 2 minutes, or until creamy. Sift the confectioner's sugar and cocoa, then gradually add them to the mixing bowl until combined. Add the milk and whisk for a final 5 minutes, or until pale and fluffy.

3 Spread the buttercream over the cooled cake, or pipe it on if you want it to look a bit fancy. Scatter over sprinkles of your choice, add any extra decorations to suit, and serve, or stash in the fridge until needed.

EMBELLISH IT ————————————————————

I sprinkled this with popping candy once and that seemed to go down well with everyone — a bit childish but a lot of fun!

ENERGY	FAT	SAT FAT	PROTEIN	CARBS	SUGARS	SALT	FIBER
375kcal	22g	12.6g	5.3g	42g	41.2g	0.2g	0.7g

PEAR & GINGER PAN TARTE TATIN

RETRO CANNED PEARS, PUNCHY JARRED GINGER & PUFF PASTRY TEAM UP TO OVER-DELIVER IN THE DESSERT STAKES

SERVES 8
PREP 20 MINUTES
COOK 25 MINUTES

2 x 15-oz cans of pear halves
in juice

1 x 12-oz jar of stem ginger
in syrup

1 vanilla pod or 1 teaspoon
vanilla bean paste

½ cup blanched hazelnuts

1 sprig of rosemary

1 x 11-oz sheet of puff pastry
(cold)

1 Preheat the oven to 350°F. Drain the juice from the pear cans into a 9 x 13-inch baking pan and place over a medium-high heat on the stove. Pour in the stem ginger syrup, then quarter or slice and add the ginger chunks.

2 Add the vanilla (halve the pod lengthwise and scrape out the seeds, if using). Boil for 10 minutes, or until reduced to the consistency of honey.

3 Stir in the pears, sprinkle in the nuts, pick, chop and scatter in the rosemary, and drizzle everything with 2 tablespoons of extra virgin olive oil.

4 Arrange the pears nicely, then unroll the pastry sheet over the top, using a spoon to help you really tuck it in at the edges. Bake for 25 minutes, or until golden and crisp, then remove the baking pan from the oven.

5 Run a palette knife around the edge of the pan, then carefully and confidently flip onto a board. Serve with crème fraîche or ice cream.

ENERGY	FAT	SAT FAT	PROTEIN	CARBS	SUGARS	SALT	FIBER
495kcal	34.4g	19.5g	6.1g	42.5g	37.5g	0.3g	1.3g

EPIC STICKY TOFFEE PUDDING

ONE OF MY FAVORITE CHILDHOOD DESSERTS MADE IN A BAKING DISH FOR ULTIMATE EASE – IT ALWAYS BRINGS A SMILE

SERVES 16
46 MINUTES

2 Earl Grey tea bags

7 oz Medjool dates

1 teaspoon baking soda

1 teaspoon ground cinnamon

1 teaspoon ground ginger

½ a nutmeg

1½ cups plus 3 tablespoons
   unsalted butter, plus extra
   for greasing

1½ cups plus 2 tablespoons
   superfine sugar

1⅔ cups packed dark
   muscovado sugar

3¾ cups self-rising flour

4 large eggs

3 tablespoons Scotch whisky

1¼ cups heavy cream

1 Preheat the oven to 325°F. Steep the tea bags in ¾ cup of boiling water, pit and add the dates, then stir in the baking soda and leave for 10 minutes.

2 Remove the tea bags, then blitz the mixture in a food processor. Add the cinnamon and ginger, grate in the nutmeg, add ¾ cup of the butter and ¾ cup of each sugar, all the flour and the eggs, then blitz again until smooth.

3 Grease a 7 x 11-inch baking dish with butter, pour in the pudding mixture, then bake for 35 minutes, or until an inserted skewer comes out clean.

4 To make the caramel sauce, put the remaining butter and sugars into a small pan, along with the whisky. Simmer for 5 minutes on a medium heat, until you get a shiny, spoonable consistency, whisking occasionally, then remove from the heat and stir in the cream.

5 As soon as the pudding is out of the oven, pour over half the caramel sauce, serving the rest on the side, for drizzling over. Delicious rippled with custard (like you see in the picture), or with whipped cream or ice cream.

ENERGY	FAT	SAT FAT	PROTEIN	CARBS	SUGARS	SALT	FIBER
485kcal	24g	14.6g	4.9g	66.1g	49.9g	0.5g	0.7g

GRILLED & ROASTED FRUIT

GIVING HUMBLE STONE FRUIT A HARD GRILL & GENTLE ROAST CREATES INCREDIBLE FLAVOR, TEXTURE & JUICES

SERVES 8
38 MINUTES

4½ lbs mixed stone fruit,
    such as peaches, nectarines,
    apricots, plums, damsons,
    cherries

1 tablespoon thick
    balsamic vinegar

liquid honey

a few sprigs of rosemary

6 small amaretti cookies

generous ½ cup shelled
    unsalted pistachios

2 cups ricotta cheese (cold)

1 lemon

1 Preheat the oven to 350°F and place a grill pan on a high heat.

2 Halve and destone the fruit, toss in a drizzle of olive oil and place cut side down on the hot grill pan for 2 minutes, or until nicely grill-marked, transferring to a snug-fitting roasting pan as you go – you'll need to work in batches. If using cherries, there's no need to grill those.

3 Drizzle the balsamic over the fruit (trust me), along with 2–4 tablespoons of honey, depending on the ripeness of your fruit, then strip and mix in the rosemary leaves. Roast for 20 minutes, or until cooked to your liking – you can make it quite stewy, or keep the fruit holding its shape.

4 Blitz the amaretti cookies and pistachios in a food processor until fine, then remove. Place the ricotta in the processor (there's no need to clean it) with 3 tablespoons of honey, finely grate in the lemon zest, add a squeeze of juice, then blitz until smooth and shiny and transfer to a serving dish.

5 To serve, spoon a little sweetened ricotta onto a plate, top with a portion of fruit, and scatter over the pistachio mixture.

EASY SWAPS ────────────────────────

This recipe is completely flexible for all seasonal stone fruit, and it even works with apples, pears, rhubarb and, dare I say it, pineapple.

ENERGY	FAT	SAT FAT	PROTEIN	CARBS	SUGARS	SALT	FIBER
260kcal	12.7g	4.1g	10.4g	27.7g	27.3g	0.2g	1.2g

RELIABLE SWEET SHORTCRUST PASTRY

MASTERING SWEET SHORTCRUST PASTRY WILL OPEN UP A WHOLE DELICIOUS WORLD OF DESSERT POSSIBILITIES

MAKES APPROX 2 LBS
10 MINUTES

4 cups all-purpose flour,
   plus extra for dusting

¾ cup confectioner's sugar

1 cup plus 2 tablespoons
   cold unsalted butter

2 large eggs

1 teaspoon vanilla bean paste

1 Sift the flour and confectioner's sugar into a large bowl. Chop the butter into cubes, then, using your fingertips, gently work it into the flour and sugar until the mixture resembles breadcrumbs (or use a food processor, if you prefer).

2 Beat the eggs with the vanilla, then use a fork or your hands to gently mix it into the flour mixture until it forms a ball of dough – add a dusting of flour if it feels too wet. It's important not to work the pastry too much at this stage or it will become elastic and chewy; we want it to be crumbly and short.

3 Cut the dough in half and either use straightaway or wrap well and pop into the fridge or freezer for another day (up to 3 days in the fridge and up to 3 months in the freezer). At this stage, you can turn the pastry into anything you wish. You can cook it free form (page 262), roll it out to line pastry cases, blind bake it and freeze, or use the cases to create something delicious (pages 264 and 266).

STRAWBERRY & BALSAMIC TART

WITH JUST 7 INGREDIENTS, THIS SCRUFFY FREE-FORM TART IS DEAD EASY BUT LOOKS & SMELLS SO STRIKING

SERVES 6
PREP 10 MINUTES
COOK 25 MINUTES

½ x Reliable sweet shortcrust
    pastry (page 260)

1 lb ripe strawberries

2 tablespoons thick
    balsamic vinegar

¼ cup superfine sugar

2 tablespoons cornstarch

¼ cup almond flour

1 egg

1 Preheat the oven to 400°F. Make the pastry, then lightly dust a large sheet of parchment paper with flour and roll it out into a rough oval shape just under ¼-inch thick. Lift the pastry on the paper onto a rimmed baking sheet.

2 Twist the stalks off the strawberries, leaving them whole, then toss with the balsamic, superfine sugar and cornstarch. Scatter the almonds across the center of the pastry, then pile the dressed strawberries on top, juice and all.

3 Use your hands to bring the pastry up at the edges to hug the strawberries, like you see in the picture, making sure the fruit is contained. Beat the egg and brush all over the exposed pastry, then bake on the bottom rack of the oven for 25 minutes, or until golden and crisp.

4 Serve right away, with ice cream, cream, custard or crème fraîche, spooning over any delicious strawberry juices from the baking sheet.

ENERGY	FAT	SAT FAT	PROTEIN	CARBS	SUGARS	SALT	FIBER
459kcal	22.9g	11.8g	7.9g	59.1g	27g	0.1g	4.5g

SWEET LITTLE INDIVIDUAL MASCARPONE TARTS

THESE CUTE TARTLETS ARE SO GOOD & YOU CAN HAVE FUN TOPPING THEM WITH ALL YOUR FAVORITE THINGS

SERVES 10–12
25 MINUTES
PLUS COOLING & DECORATING

½ x Reliable sweet shortcrust pastry (page 260)

2–4 tablespoons confectioner's sugar

2½ cups mascarpone cheese

1 teaspoon vanilla bean paste

toppings of your choice (see step 4)

1 Preheat the oven to 350°F. Make the pastry, then, on a lightly flour-dusted surface, roll out to ⅛-inch thick. Cut out circles ½ inch larger than your pans — this quantity of pastry makes 10 x 8-inch tartlets if you use mini tart pans, or 12 tartlets if you use a 12-cup muffin pan pan — rerolling and cutting any offcuts, as needed.

2 Line each pan or cup with the pastry. Line the pastry with scrunched-up damp parchment paper, fill with dried rice and blind bake in the center of the oven for 15 minutes, then remove the paper and rice and bake for a final 5 minutes, or until golden and crisp. Leave to cool.

3 Sift the confectioner's sugar (depending on the sweetness of your toppings), mix into the mascarpone with the vanilla, then divide between the cooled tart cases.

4 Now for the fun bit — the toppings! Go to town with fresh seasonal, canned or frozen fruit, jams, curds, compotes, nut butters, melted or shaved chocolate and nuts. Go classy, logical, naughty or nostalgic, whatever you desire! Or you could even set up a station of sweet topping treats and let your guests build their own.

ENERGY	FAT	SAT FAT	PROTEIN	CARBS	SUGARS	SALT	FIBER
362kcal	4.6g	25.5g	9.4g	25.5g	9.4g	0.1g	0.6g

CHERRY CHOCOLATE FRANGIPANE PIE

CHERRIES & CHOCOLATE ARE THE BEST OF FRIENDS; ADD SWEET CRUMBLY PASTRY & YOU REALLY CAN'T GO WRONG

SERVES 14
PREP 50 MINUTES
COOK 1 HOUR
PLUS COOLING

1 x Reliable sweet shortcrust pastry (page 260)

1 lb frozen pitted cherries

3 tablespoons cornstarch

¾ cup superfine sugar

½ an orange

optional: 3 tablespoons Scotch whisky

7 tablespoons soft unsalted butter

3 large eggs

1 cup almond flour

1 tablespoon all-purpose flour

3 tablespoons unsweetened cocoa powder

1 tablespoon demerara sugar

1 Preheat the oven to 350°F. Make the pastry, then roll out the first half on a flour-dusted surface to just under ¼-inch thick. Loosely roll it up around the rolling pin and unroll over a 10-inch loose-bottomed tart pan, then gently ease into the sides, trimming any excess. Chill in the fridge for 15 minutes.

2 In a small pan, mix the frozen cherries, cornstarch, ⅓ cup of superfine sugar, the orange zest and juice, and the whisky, if using. Bring to a boil and simmer for just 2 minutes, or until thickened, then leave to cool.

3 Line your pastry shell with a large sheet of scrunched-up damp parchment paper, pushing it right into the sides. Fill with dried rice and blind bake in the center of the oven for 15 minutes. Carefully remove the paper and rice and bake for a further 5 minutes.

4 Roll out the remaining pastry to just under ¼-inch thick, cut into strips, cover loosely to prevent them drying out and set aside.

5 For the frangipane, beat the soft butter and the remaining superfine sugar together, then mix in 2 eggs, the almond flour, all-purpose flour and cocoa powder, and spread across the base of the pastry case.

6 Pour over the cooled cherries, spreading them right to the edges, then lay over the pastry strips, randomly interlacing them to mostly cover the filling and pressing down at the edges to seal. Trim any excess, beat the remaining egg and eggwash the top of the pie, then sprinkle over the demerara sugar.

7 Bake in the center of the oven for 40 minutes, or until golden and crisp. Let rest for 20 minutes before serving.

ENERGY	FAT	SAT FAT	PROTEIN	CARBS	SUGARS	SALT	FIBER
494kcal	27.6g	14.3g	8.3g	56.9g	26.8g	0.1g	1.4g

SIMPLY HELPFUL

CELEBRATE QUALITY & SEASONALITY

As is often the case in cooking, using quality ingredients really does make a difference to the success of the recipes. I've tried to keep the number of ingredients under control, so I'm hoping that will give you the excuse to trade up where you can, buying the best veggies, fish or meat you can find. Also, remember that shopping in season always allows your food to be more delicious and more affordable. When it comes to veg and fruit, remember to give everything a nice wash before you start cooking, especially if you're using stuff raw. Ingredients that are noticeably more delicious when you choose the best quality are sausages, cured meats, cheese, jarred beans and chickpeas, canned plum tomatoes, crunchy peanut & sesame chili oil, sea salt, honey and dark chocolate.

FOCUSING ON FISH & SEAFOOD

Fish and seafood are an incredibly delicious source of protein but literally the minute they're caught they start to deteriorate in freshness, so you want to buy them as close to the day of your meal as you can – I wouldn't endorse them being stored in the fridge for days, you're better off with frozen if that's the case. I recommend planning your fish and seafood dinners around your shopping days. Make sure you choose responsibly sourced fish and seafood – look for the MSC logo, or talk to your fishmonger and take their advice. Try to mix up your choices, choosing seasonal, sustainable options as they're available. If you can only find farmed fish, make sure you look for the ASC logo to ensure your fish is responsibly sourced.

MEAT & EGGS

When it comes to meat, of course I'm going to endorse higher-welfare farming practices, like organic or free-range. Animals should be raised well and free to roam, display natural behaviors and live a stress-free healthy life. Like most things, you pay more for quality. I'm always a believer that if you take a couple of minutes to plan your weekly menus, you can be clever about using cheaper cuts of meat, or you could try cooking some of my meat-reduced and vegetarian dishes, which should give you the opportunity to trade up to quality proteins when you do choose them. For a few of the cuts of meat in this book, you might like to go to a butcher, and I cannot recommend this enough. They can be so helpful: they can order stuff in especially for you and can ensure you have the exact weights you need. Unless essential to a recipe we don't specify egg sizes. Hens naturally lay a variety of sizes of egg, so look for mixed-size boxes when shopping to support the best possible welfare standards. When it comes to eggs and anything containing egg, such as pasta or mayonnaise, always choose free-range or organic.

DIAL UP YOUR DAIRY

With staple dairy products, like milk, yogurt and butter, please trade up to organic if you can. Unlike meat, it is only slightly more expensive and I couldn't recommend it enough, if it's available to you. Every time you buy organic, you vote for a better food system that supports the highest standards of animal welfare, where both cows and land are well looked after.

KITCHEN NOTES

FRIDGE ORGANIZATION

When juggling space in the fridge, remember that raw meat and fish should be well wrapped and placed on the bottom shelf to avoid cross-contamination. Any food that is ready to eat, whether it's cooked or it doesn't need to be cooked, should be stored on a higher shelf.

THE FREEZER IS YOUR BEST FRIEND

For busy people, without doubt your freezer, if stocked correctly, is your closest ally. There are just a few basic rules when it comes to really utilizing it well. If you're batch-cooking, remember to let food cool thoroughly before freezing – break it down into portions so it cools quicker, and get it into the freezer within 2 hours. Make sure everything is well wrapped, and labeled for future reference. Thaw in the fridge before use, and use within 48 hours. If you've frozen cooked food, don't freeze it again after reheating or thawing it. Nutritionally speaking, freezing veg and fruit quickly after harvesting retains the nutritional value very efficiently, often trumping fresh equivalents that have been stuck in the supply chain for a while. You will see me using frozen veg (which I love!) often in these recipes – it's super-convenient and widely available.

MAXIMIZING FLAVOR

In this book I use a lot of what I like to call "flavor bombs": widely available ingredients that allow you to add big bonus flavor, fast. Much-loved pastes include harissa, miso, gochujang, pesto, tahini and many curry pastes. Useful things in brine include jarred roasted red peppers, olives and capers. Helpful things in oil: anchovies, artichoke hearts and sun-dried tomatoes. These all really bolster the flavor of a dish in just one super-charged ingredient. I love spices and blends like paprika, dukkah and curry powder, to name a few, as well as nuts, seeds and dried fruit; and cracking condiments, such as mustards, chili oils, chili sauces and mango chutney. They all work so hard on the flavor front. These items guarantee flavor and consistency, educate your palate and save hours of time in preparation. Most are non-perishable, which means you're not under pressure to use them up super-quickly.

BIGGING UP FRESH HERBS

Fresh herbs are a gift to any cook. Instead of buying them, why not grow them yourself in the garden or in a pot on your windowsill? Herbs allow you to add single-minded flavor to a dish, without the need to over-season, which is good for everyone. They're also packed with all sorts of incredible qualities on the nutritional front – we like that. And don't forget dried herbs – they're not a compromise for fresh, they're just different. Wonderfully, they still retain a huge amount of nutritional value, but it's the dramatic change in flavor that is useful to us cooks. Plus, they're non-perishable and super-convenient to have ready and raring to go. The ones I always have in my pantry are oregano, dill, rosemary, mint and thyme, to name just a few.

OVEN & AIR FRYER LOVIN'

All recipes are tested in fan ovens in °C and then converted to °F for this book – find conversions for conventional and gas ovens online. Recipes that use an air fryer were tested in a 4.2-liter (approximately 4.4 quart) air fryer – all air fryers are different, so results may vary.

A NOTE FROM JAMIE'S NUTRITION TEAM

Our job is to make sure that Jamie can be super-creative, while also ensuring that all recipes meet our guidelines. Every book has a different brief, and *Simply Jamie* is about making mealtimes easier, every day of the week. With the exception of the Delicious Desserts chapter and some of the meal components, like dressings, 70% of the recipes fit into our everyday food guidelines. In some cases, recipes aren't complete meals, so you'll need to balance out your mealtimes with what's lacking – the info that follows below will help you with this. For clarity and so that you can make informed choices, we've presented easy-to-read nutrition info for each dish on the recipe page (displayed per serving). We also want to inspire a more sustainable way of eating, so 65% of the recipes are either meat-free or meat-reduced (meaning they contain at least 30% less meat than a regular portion size). Food is fun, joyful and creative – it gives us energy and plays a crucial role in keeping our bodies healthy. Remember, a nutritious, varied and balanced diet and regular exercise are the keys to a healthier lifestyle. We don't label foods as "good" or "bad" – there's a place for everything. We encourage an understanding of the difference between nutritious foods for everyday consumption and those to be enjoyed occasionally. For more info about our guidelines and how we analyze recipes, please visit jamieoliver.com/nutrition.

Rozzie Batchelar – Senior Nutritionist, RNutr (food)

A BIT ABOUT BALANCE

Balance is key when it comes to eating well. Balance your plate right and keep your portion control in check, and you can be confident that you're giving yourself a great start on the path to good health. It's important to consume a variety of foods to ensure we get the nutrients our bodies need to stay healthy. You don't have to be spot-on every day – just try to get your balance right across the week. If you eat meat and fish, as a general guide for main meals you want at least two portions of fish a week, one of which should be oily. Split the rest of the week's main meals between brilliant plant-based meals, some poultry and a little red meat. An all-vegetarian diet can be perfectly healthy, too.

WHAT'S THE BALANCE

The UK government's Eatwell Guide shows us what a healthy balance of food looks like. The figures below indicate the proportion of each food group that's recommended across the day.

THE FIVE FOOD GROUPS (UK)	PROPORTION
Vegetables & fruit	40%
Starchy carbohydrates (bread, rice, potatoes, pasta)	38%
Protein (lean meat, fish, eggs, beans, other non-dairy sources)	12%
Dairy foods, milk & dairy alternatives	8%
Unsaturated fats (such as oils)	1%
AND DON'T FORGET TO DRINK PLENTY OF WATER, TOO	

Try to only consume foods and drinks high in fat, salt or sugar occasionally.

VEGETABLES & FRUIT

To live a good, healthy life, vegetables and fruit should sit right at the heart of your diet. Veg and fruit come in all kinds of colors, shapes, sizes, flavors and textures, and contain different vitamins and minerals, which each play a part in keeping our bodies healthy and optimal, so variety is key. Eat the rainbow, mixing up your choices as much as you can and embracing the seasons so you're getting produce at its best and its most nutritious. As an absolute minimum, aim for at least five portions of fresh, frozen or canned veg and fruit every day of the week, enjoying more wherever possible. 80g (3 oz) (or a large handful) counts as one portion. You can also count one 30g (1 oz) portion of dried fruit, one 80g (3 oz) portion of beans or legumes, and 150ml (⅔ cup) of unsweetened veg or fruit juice per day.

STARCHY CARBOHYDRATES

Carbs provide us with a large proportion of the energy needed to make our bodies move, and to ensure our organs have the fuel they need to function. When you can, choose fiber-rich whole grain and whole wheat varieties. 260g is the recommended daily amount of carbohydrates for the average adult, with up to 90g coming from total sugars, which include natural sugars found in whole fruit, milk and milk products, and no more than 30g of free sugars. Free sugars are those added to food and drink, including sugar found in honey, syrups, fruit juice and smoothies. Fiber is classified as a carbohydrate and is mainly found in plant-based foods such as whole grains, veg and fruit. It helps to keep our digestive systems healthy, control our blood-sugar levels and maintain healthy cholesterol levels. Adults should be aiming for at least 30g of fiber each day.

PROTEIN

Think of protein as the building blocks of our bodies – it's used for everything that's important to how we grow and repair. Try to vary your proteins to include more beans and legumes, and two sources of sustainably sourced fish per week (one of which is oily), and reduce red and processed meat if your diet is high in these. Choose lean cuts of animal-based protein where you can.

Beans, peas and lentils are great alternatives to meat because they're naturally low in fat and, as well as protein, they contain fiber and some vitamins and minerals. Other nutritious protein sources include tofu, eggs, nuts and seeds. Variety is key! The requirement for an average woman aged 19 to 50 is 45g per day, with 55g for men in the same age bracket.

DAIRY FOODS, MILK & DAIRY ALTERNATIVES

This food group offers an amazing array of nutrients when eaten in the right amounts. Favor organic dairy milk and yogurt, and small amounts of cheese, in this category; the lower-fat varieties (with no added sugar) are equally brilliant and worth embracing. If opting for plant-based versions, I think it's great that we have choice, but it's really important to look for unsweetened fortified options that have added calcium, iodine and vitamin B12 in the ingredients list, to avoid missing out on the key nutrients provided by dairy milk.

UNSATURATED FATS

While we only need small amounts, we do require healthier fats. Choose unsaturated sources where you can, such as olive and liquid vegetable oils, nuts, seeds, avocado and omega-3 rich oily fish. Generally speaking, it's recommended that the average woman has no more than 70g of fat per day, with less than 20g of that from saturated fat, and the average man no more than 90g, with less than 30g from saturated fat.

DRINK PLENTY OF WATER

To be the best you can be, stay hydrated. Water is essential to life, and to every function of the human body! In general, women aged 14 and over need at least 2 liters (8 cups) per day and men in the same age bracket need at least 2.5 liters (10 cups) per day.

ENERGY & NUTRITION INFO

The average woman needs 2,000 calories per day, while the average man needs roughly 2,500. These figures are a rough guide, and what we eat needs to be considered in relation to factors like your age, build, lifestyle and activity levels.

SIMPLY

In all circumstances in life, we're often boosted and made better by the people around us, and that's certainly true of the incredible team that supports me in the creation, production and promotion of my cookbooks. Every soul involved brings something extra to the process, and being lucky enough to work with people whose strengths complement mine and fill in the gaps is something I never take for granted. So, as ever, let me begin with a big expression of gratitude to all those named on these pages.

Kicking things off is my cherished food team, who play a vital role in recipe creation, relentless recipe testing, and support me on the photo shoots that bring my books to life. They're given constancy by Ginny Rolfe, who is as much a part of the furniture as me, and my second food brain. Big love as well to super-talented Joss Herd, Anna Helm Baxter, Ben Slater, Rachel Young, Sharon Sharpe, Maggie Musmar, Becky Wheeldon, Laura McLeish, Tilly Wilson and Helen Martin. My faithful food team extensions are genius brain Pete Begg and steadfast Bobby Sebire, who I'm ever so thankful for. And we're lucky enough to have a much-loved freelance food team family, too. Respect to Maddie Rix, Isla Murray, Sophie Mackinnon, Hattie Arnold, Holly Cowgill, George Stocks and Christina Mackenzie.

Inspiring me to ground my books in solid nutrition and clever thinking around health and nutrition is my Senior Nutritionist Rozzie "cake queen" Batchelar, and providing the technical intel on food safety, food standards, farming and ethics is Lucinda Cobb.

Over on words (and beyond!), big love to my wonderful Editor-in-Chief Rebecca Verity, to lovely Beth Stroud, Jade Melling, Ruth Tebby and the rest of the team. Thank you for what you do, with patience and enthusiasm.

Shout-out to my style icon and Creative Director James Verity, to new-talent-in-the-mix Davina Mistry and the rest of the design team – you smashed the brief.

On photography, it's been a joy and a pleasure to work solely with my dear friend David Loftus on this one. Thank you for helping this book have its own distinctive and beautiful look. Thank you also to his assistant Richard Bowyer for the support and the LOLs.

Over at my publisher, Penguin Random House, there are an incredible number of important people to thank. It's a big jigsaw of a process and I have a lot of respect for the intricacies of what you all do. To the OGs, Tom Weldon and Louise Moore, and to Elizabeth Smith,

THANKS

Clare Parker, Tom Troughton, Ella Watkins, Alicia Jackson, Juliette Butler, Katherine Tibbals, Lee Motley, Sarah Fraser, Nick Lowndes, Christina Ellicott, Laura Garrod, Kelly Mason, Emma Carter, Hannah Padgham, Chris Wyatt, Tracy Orchard, Chantal Noel, Anjali Nathani, Kate Reiners, Tyra Burr, Joanna Whitehead, Madeleine Stephenson, Lee-Anne Williams, Jessica Meredeen, Sarah Porter, Grace Dellar, Stuart Anderson, Anna Curvis, Akua Akowuah, Samantha Waide, Richard Rowlands and Carrie Anderson.

Not forgetting ever-faithful Annie Lee, as well as Jill Cole, Emma Horton and Ruth Ellis.

Back at JO HQ, I'm always thankful for the passionate support my books get from the whole business. Calling out those who are directly involved, thank you to the marketing and PR crew, Rosalind Godber, Michelle Dam, Clare Duffy, Tamsyn Zeitsman and Lydia Waller. Thank you to Letitia Becher, Bryony Palmer and the social team, Rich Herd and the rest of the VPU. In finance, big up Pamela Lovelock, Therese MacDermott and John Dewar. Respect to Giovanna Milia and the legal team, and of course to everyone else, including the personnel, operations, IT, P&D and facilities teams.

I have a loyal and dedicated group of office testers, who cook up these recipes at home to make sure they really do work, so much love to all of you guys.

A special thank you to my CEO Kevin Styles, my illustrious Deputy Louise Holland, my brilliant Media MD Zoe Collins, and my favorite EA Ali Solway.

Over on the TV side – and I just know you're going to love the show that goes with this book – big thanks and love to the cornerstones of my TV world who bring energy and optimism, Sean Moxhay, Sam Beddoes and Katie Millard. To Delia Williams, Ed St Giles, Amanda Doig-Moore and Renzo Luzardo. And to Cliff Evans, Dave Minchin, Callum Woodward, Mike Sarah and Prarthana Peterarulthas. Thank you to Tobie Tripp for the tunes. And to Tim Hancock and the team at Channel 4, plus the whole Fremantle crew – you know who you are!

Big love as well to lovely Julia Bell, Lima O'Donnell and Violet Cannon; thank you for all that you do.

And to my family, Jools, Pops, Daisy, Petal, Buds and River, to Mum and Dad, to Gennaro, and the rest of the big old bunch, thank you for being with me on this ride. Much love.

INDEX

Recipes marked V are suitable for vegetarians; in some instances you'll need to swap in a vegetarian alternative to cheese such as Parmesan.

A ----------------------------

B ----------------------------

D –

For a quick reference list of all the vegetarian, vegan, dairy-free and gluten-free recipes in this book, visit:
jamieoliver.com/SimplyJamie/reference

THE JAMIE OLIVER COLLECTION

HUNGRY FOR MORE?

For handy nutrition advice, as well as videos, features, hints, tricks and tips on all sorts of different subjects, loads of brilliant recipes, plus much more, check out

JAMIEOLIVER.COM   #SIMPLYJAMIE

Photography by David Loftus

Designed by Jamie Oliver Limited

Color reproduction by Altaimage Ltd

jamieoliver.com
www.flatironbooks.com

The Library of Congress Cataloging-in-Publication Data is available upon request.

ISBN 978-1-250-37400-4 (paper over board)
ISBN 978-1-250-37401-1 (ebook)

Our books may be purchased in bulk for promotional, educational, or business use. Please contact your local bookseller or the Macmillan Corporate and Premium Sales Department at 1-800-221-7945, extension 5442, or by email at MacmillanSpecialMarkets@macmillan.com.

First published in the United Kingdom in 2024 by Penguin Michael Joseph, part of the Penguin Random House group of companies

First U.S. Edition: 2025

Printed in Italy by Graphicom

10 9 8 7 6 5 4 3 2 1

BIG LOVE

Thank you for buying my cookbook – by doing so you're contributing to my Ministry of Food program, which is on a mission to teach 1 million people to cook by 2030.

Find out more: jamieoliver.com